Author Ke
1070⁄
˙ Rolla, Mo. 65401

1-573-465-0275
kenvic58@embarqmail.com

GOD CALLED MY NAME

Delivered From The Slime Pit Of Hell

"I was a hard nut to Crack."

I Have Been Set Free

By KENNETH CAMPBELL

FORWARD

In my 30 + years of full time ministry, I have encountered few men who were actually sincerely working in the fields of harvest at a street level. While this statement may seem strange to you at the onset, let me somewhat clarify. There are untold numbers of individuals that are "building" a ministry or church and so they have that primary motivation. They clamor for a pulpit handing out their cards, tapes, and DVDs at every opportunity; they attend Christian events such as conventions, rallies, and revivals in attempts to further their ministry or church work. While this is indeed an honorable work, somewhere the actual harvest work in the fields suffers tremendously. However, in the fields of harvest, where the rubber meets the road, where there are boots on the ground in the actual personal reaching out to the lost, I have encountered few individuals personally laboring with one motivation and one motivation alone. They reach the souls of the lost with the Gospel of our Beloved Lord of Life – Yeshua – Jesus – Son of the True and Living God. I encountered these two men actually laboring while in the fields of harvest. Kenneth Campbell is such a man.

His heart and his message is True and bears with it deliverance from the slim pits of hell to being set free, if you will but hear his heart felt cry of "I am free!" "I am free!"

While there are many encounters I have been blessed to share with this man of Truth, I want to share with you but one.

It was a cold day with ice on the ground and walkways in this particular apartment complex. As it was somewhat misting freezing ice, I found myself at Kenneth's side. In his frustration, so few would listen as he went door to door with the love of Christ, coupled with the thought that so very many were horribly bound in their pain and "going to hell" as he put it, he asked if we could pray. I immediately said yes and without hesitation or concern he knelt on the ice with his head bowed eager to call out for the souls of this people. Our prayers were solid and straight forward calling out for the souls to come to know the love of a just God and be set free. Upon completion, we arose and Kenneth's smiling face filled me as he hugged me and he disappeared into the weather to find another place, another building, and another soul that might listen and be set free.

This is Kenneth's true nature, his true heart, and it is the heart of his message in this book that you now read.

Kenneth is an elderly man and he and his precious wife Vickie have worked hard all of their lives. They live in a nice, but modest, home. Yet, their lives are focused on touching everyone that they can with the love of God. From the children to the "hardest nuts to crack", you will find that Kenneth and Vickie are continually reaching out with the message and helping hand of our Beloved Christ Jesus so that one more might be set free.

"I am FREE!" he shouts at the top of his lungs. "Free!"

Tommy L. Tibbetts
International author and Founder of Deeper Life
Ministries / Hardcore International Ministries

*"And they have overcome (conquered) him (Satan
the Accuser of the brethren, he who keeps bringing
before our God charges against them day and night)
by the blood of the Lamb and but the utterance of
their testimony, for they did not love and cling to life
even when faced with death (holding their lives cheap
till they die for their witnessing)."*
Revelations 12: 10-11 Amplified Bible

ACKNOWLEDGMENTS

First, to Jesus Christ for the sacrifice He made for me on Calvary. For saving my soul, setting me free and giving me a forever home in heaven.

To Jennifer Gray, for her work of typing and figuring out my handwriting.

To Janna Reilly-Cox, for her help in organizing my rambling thoughts.

To everyone who shared the incredible testimonies which gave me the desire to share them with others.

To my wife of over 50 years, who has supported me in all my endeavors, from house building to preaching.

TABLE OF CONTENTS

MY STORY...13
TESTIMONIES 29
ON LIGHT 30
GOD CALLED 34
ON ANGELS 37
ON VISIONS 43
ON OUT OF BODY 49
ON MIRACLES...51
ON HELL...62
ON PRAYER 65
ON PROTECTION..73
RIGHT PLACE – RIGHT TIME...........................81
GOD'S SENSE OF HUMOR 86
GOD'S PLAN 89
HATE 94
VICKIE'S VIEW 96
AFTER THOUGHTS 97
FINAL THOUGHTS 99

MY STORY-KENNETH CAMPBELL

I was born in 1936 during the depression. Our home had no electricity or running water until I was 10-12 years old. We lived in the poor part of Rolla, Missouri. It was over a mile to school and everyone walked back then. My Dad worked at the shoe factory and my Mom worked at Busy Bee Laundry. We had a 1931 Model "A" Ford and used it to haul the wood we cut with a crosscut saw. I had three brothers, one of which died at six weeks of age. I would try to catch rabbits, squirrels and fish in the creeks and ponds to help provide food for the family. We lived on the edge of town, so I was out in the woods almost every day. My brother Bob and I also picked blackberries for Mom to can or to sell for extra money. My two older brothers took care of me while our parents were working. The eldest brother, Lowell, was very smart. Since we didn't have many toys, if I wanted something to play with, he would just make it. My other brother, Bob, and I were close. He became very ill when his appendix burst and he almost lost his life.

When I was about 15 years old, I started working on a delivery truck earning $3 a day. The next summer I worked at the shoe factory for seventy-five cents an hour. The following year, I started at the grocery store and worked

36 hours a week while continuing school. I graduated from High School in 1954 and then started a small business fixing tires and selling them to local gas stations. Business wasn't as good as I thought it would be and I ended up working again at the shoe factory.

During this time, my two older brothers, Lowell and Bob, went into the Armed services. Lowell went into the Air Force for four years and Bob into the Army for two. When each of them got out, they attended MSM (Missouri School of Mines). I was saving my money from working at the shoe factory and managed to buy two building lots in the shoe factory addition for $700. Knowing I didn't want to work making shoes for the rest of my life, I quit and joined the Air Force.

While in St. Louis taking care of the admission process, I was sent to an office for my I.D. tags. When asked whether I was Protestant or Catholic, I said, "Neither, I guess, because I don't go to church." I told her some of my friends are Catholic and told her I went to a Baptist church when I was five years old. So we agreed I must be a Protestant. I know now that she didn't want to write "atheist" on my tags. I was sent to Texas for Basic Training and during that time, I went to church every Sunday. After training, my first duty station was Kessler Air Force Base in Mississippi. I would often drive back to Rolla for visits. One night on my way back to base, I picked up a hitchhiker, hoping that he would keep me awake on the long drive. We talked for a while, but it wasn't long before he was fast asleep. The next thing I knew, I found myself on the wrong side of the road, facing two bright lights. I had nodded off. I realize now that God had a plan for me, even then.

During one of my visits home, I met a girl who was also stationed at the Air Base, and took her to meet my new friends there. We all started to attend a Baptist church in Biloxi and then another one in Pascagoula where I dated the pastor's daughter a few times. At the end of my 36 weeks at Kessler, the time for exams came around. Charles was encouraging me to study so we could move on to Kansas City together. I really didn't care if I passed or not, but God did. It was part of His plan. I ended up passing the exam by half a point and Charles and I moved on to Kansas. We got an apartment off Central Ave and settled in. I found I wasn't a very good cook. I made some gravy one day and it was about like Jell-O. You could slice it or put it on toast or you could play with it like silly putty. Needless to say, it didn't taste as good as Jell-O.

Charles and I would often go sightseeing in my '51 Mercury. In those days, you could buy a gallon of gas for about 20 cents. Sometimes during a gas war, you could get gas for as low as 13 cents a gallon. One evening we met a bright red and white Model A Ford driven by a longhaired girl. I said to Charles, "Did you see that?"

He said, "I saw it, but I don't believe it."

"I thought I would never marry, but she couldn't be all bad, driving a Model A. I just might marry her, if I ever meet her," I said.

The following Sunday, being tired of my own bad cooking, I stopped in to a local Café some guys had told me about. When I walked in, the aromas melted my heart. I was in love with the cook, even though I hadn't seen her. The food looked and smelled like my Mom used to make and I couldn't decide what mouth-watering dish to choose. After I had finished off the delicious roast beef, mashed potatoes and gravy, my waitress asked if I would like some fresh strawberries and ice cream. After confirming that I would, she asked if I wanted anything else. Although I was bashful in those days, I blurted, "Would you consider going out with me?" She came back with the question, "Will you go to church with me tonight?" I said "yes" as if I had been going to church all my life.

She gave me directions to the church and said she would meet me there at 6:00 pm. I met her Mom and Dad and after the service was over, her Dad said I could drive her home. She lived on five acres at the edge of town and I knew I wouldn't have been able to find it on my own. When I pulled up in the driveway, there sat a red and white Model A Ford. I asked who it belonged to and she said, "Me." Of all the cafés in Kansas City, I went to the one she worked in. What are the odds that I would sit down in front of the girl I said I would marry if I ever met her? Even her birth date is special. Vickie and my Mother were both born on July 18th. It was all in God's plan.

Before Vickie and I were married, I started building a house on one of the lots I had purchased with my shoe factory money. I contracted Willis Pierce to build for me and he and my Dad worked on it through the fall of 1957. The following spring, I brought Vickie home to meet my folks and she helped me work on the inside of the house and prepared it to be rented out. After we were married, I was transferred to St. Paul, Minnesota, bought a trailer and lived on the Army post there for almost two years. By the time I got out of the Air Force in 1960, we had paid off both the house and our trailer. We moved the trailer and ourselves back to Rolla and a few months later started building another house on the second lot I owned. Vickie continued to work at the U.S. Geological Survey for the next few years while I worked at the U.S. Bureau of Mines and sold insurance in the evening.

In 1961, we were attending Second Baptist Church and Vickie was teaching Sunday school there. My brother Lowell had returned to Rolla and we started building houses. Within a few years, Vickie and I had quit our jobs and were building houses full time. She could paint, trowel concrete, lay ceramic tile and varnish floors. She even helped me with the wiring. Vickie took care of all the bookwork and bills.

I wouldn't have made it in this business without her. Even today, I am reminded of what a blessing she has been to all of us; when I walk into our Pastor Leroy's office at the church, I look down at the floor she laid over 35 years ago.

On a cold winter day in 1963, Vickie and I went to check on one of our rental houses and found something wrong on the ridge of the roof. I got a ladder and climbed up to repair it. Even though there was snow in spots, I thought if I stayed on the ridge, I would be okay. When I turned, however, I slipped, fell and started sliding towards the edge. I knew there was a concrete porch under me and was aware of the injuries I would sustain, if I landed there. At the last moment of my fall, I grabbed the edge and jumped as far as I could. I landed on the frozen yard about fifteen feet away. I hit so hard, my legs buckled under me, but I got up without any broken bones. God and His angels had a hand on me.

A few years later, I earned my pilot's license and we decide to rent a plane and fly to visit friends in Mattoon, Illinois. As we flew over the arch in St. Louis, the weather started getting bad. We should have turned back at that point, but I'm kind of stubborn. The clouds opened up and I could see clear sky ahead of me. But soon I was surrounded by clouds again and couldn't see the ground. I told Vickie that I would have to go down through the clouds before too long, knowing we were getting close to the airport. I asked her to watch the two dials on her side of the dash and I would watch two more on my side. We were about 50 feet above a cornfield so I gained a little altitude and began to see the streets and buildings of Mattoon. I made a correction to the southeast, saw some black asphalt and landed the plane. We were in the parking lot of the airport. There was no way I could have landed that plane past all the lines and towers if God hadn't been guiding me.

Vickie and I had been talking about going to Australia for a few years and finally booked passage on a freighter for a cost of $745 each. We had an auction and sold almost everything we owned. We kept a Trail 90 motorcycle, a few guns, Vickie's dishes and sewing machine and a couple of barrels of clothes. We packed our suitcases and headed to San Francisco, California with the ride provided by Vickie's Mom and Aunt Ellen. We boarded the Lloyd Bakke, a Norwegian ship with a Chinese crew. The freighter was 573 ft long and 65 ft. wide. It took twelve passengers along with a crew of fifty. The food was wonderful and stewards cleaned our room all 42 days of the crossing. Our first port of call was at the 16-day mark and took us to Hong Kong. The second was 20 miles from the capitol of Kuala Lumpur. We had two more stops in Australia before coming to our final destination in Perth. We met many interesting people on our voyage including Charles and Isabel Hyne, who lived sixty miles north of Perth. Since I was feeling sick, we stayed for about a week at a local hotel the Hynes told us about before moving on.

We purchased a Volkswagen van and started our tour. We drove along the coast and then took a break, rented a plane and flew around Bunbury. We then continued, once again, in the van and followed the coast to the east. We saw a light-house and stopped to sit on the rocks below it and watched the waves. A man warned us to move up higher due to the King Waves. He said the waves in that area were known to break at the bottom of the lighthouse that was 90 ft. above the water. We headed further east and started seeing huge trees. We found one with a tower on the top with steel pins and wooden pegs to climb it. So I did. It was 212 ft. high and when I got to the top and looked out upon the shorter trees, it looked like a green lawn below. We got on the road again, and headed back to Perth and then onward north to visit Charles and Isabel's home. I was still feeling sick during our visit and noticed I was losing weight. I didn't think much about this and we hit the road again up the west coast of

Australia. One morning as we started out, we got stuck in the sand. It was all the way up to the bumper and frame on one side. I told Vickie that I thought I could pick up the van far enough for her to place flat rocks in the ruts. She gathered some rocks and when ready, I got a hold of the smooth part of the bumper and picked it up enough for her to get the rocks under the tire. We started the van and were able to pull out on the road. About fifteen miles down the road, I said to her, "How did I do that?" She replied, "I don't know." Here I was sick, down to 130 lbs, with a van full of luggage, fuel and small appliances. Angels must have helped me lift that van. Towards the end of our road trip, we discovered oil running out of the engine; we had it repaired only to have it happen again. Both times it happened we were driving into a town. With the towns in that area being over 240 miles apart, if it had happened on the road, we may have lost our lives to dehydration or heat stroke. Before selling our van, we saw Ayers Rock, Alice Springs and the Great Barrier Reef, along with the east coast to Sydney and Melbourne.

We flew to New Zealand and toured both the North and South Islands in a rental car. In one day, we flew from New Zealand, across the Tasman Sea, across Australia, across the Indian Ocean and landed in Madagascar. Our next flight took us to Johannesburg, South Africa where we were charged by an elephant while traveling in a van during a photo safari in Kruger Park. A woman on our safari happened to be a nurse and noticed that I wasn't feeling well. She offered advice on what to eat and drink. I was losing weight and starting to feel very weak. Vickie took me to a doctor who prescribed some pills for me, but they made no difference. I was still losing weight and was starting to feel very weak. We started north by plane from South Africa and went to Victoria Falls. The next country was in a war and we didn't know if we were going to get out of that country. I was getting very sick.

Next, we traveled to the Holy Land and stayed in a hotel in Tel Aviv. We ventured out to Jerusalem and saw many temples and churches as well as the Bethlehem Church built over the stable where Jesus was born. We hired a taxi driver to take us to see all the things of interest to us for a flat fee of $30. Excitedly, we jumped into the back of a big, black Mercedes and saw many sites including the Dead Sea and Jericho. I wondered at the time, why we didn't see many tourists. We took a tour on a bus around some more of the country. We were in Golan Heights in 1972. The guide told me to not leave the sidewalk because last night 4 people had been killed by land mines right there. I found out later that there was a war going on.

I was getting weaker by the day and told Vickie that I wanted to go home. I even had to be helped up three steps into a building by an elderly man. At the time, I thought I was going to die and didn't want to do so in Israel. We went to the TWA office and requested the earliest flight possible. The next morning our flight was called and we walked across the tarmac to board the plane. The plane was huge and as I looked up at all those steps, I feared I was not going to make it. I told Vickie that if she carried the bags, I might be able to get up the steps. It was the struggle of my life, but I made it. The pilot made an announcement that welcomed all 30 passengers. He said there were 33 stewards to take care of us. We stretched out across the seats and headed north to Germany. Then the plane landed in New York, late the next evening, and we had to spend the night because our connecting flight to St. Louis had already left.

The next morning we boarded another plane and arrived in St. Louis around noon. My brother Lowell and his wife Gladys were at the terminal waiting for us. As I walked up to them, they didn't even recognize me. They saw Vickie and looked back at me in disbelief. I was very sick and didn't know why.

When we got to my parent's house, Mom had fixed a big meal for us. I couldn't eat at all; everything tasted bad. Dad was trying to get me to go deer hunting and I finally relented. I was so weak; I could barely carry the gun. The next morning Dad insisted we hunt again. We rode around in the truck looking for deer and I ended up shooting a big buck from the passenger side. We both walked out to where I shot it and saw blood in the snow. I tried to talk him out of it, but Dad insisted on going to find it. I bent down to look at the tracks and when I stood up, I couldn't see. I stood still for a few minutes and then started getting my sight back. When Dad returned, we went home immediately. The next day, I went to see a doctor who referred me to one in St. Louis. I ended up in the hospital where they took my blood pressure and found it at 80/30. Later that day, after many tests, a doctor came in and told me he knew what was wrong with me. I had Addison's disease, the same thing John F. Kennedy was diagnosed with. The doctor told me that I would probably not be able to do any physical labor and would be on medication the rest of my life.

Thirty-five years after hearing my diagnosis, I've built almost 300 houses, visited Canada 20-30 times, Alaska four times and went back to Australia and New Zealand. We've been to Japan and South America and boated down the Yukon River five times. I got to see how the Indians and Eskimos lived, caught salmon in nets and fish wheels and road with a bush pilot to Bethel, Alaska on the Bering Sea. I rode a DC-3 from Fairbanks to Whitehorse and have been all over the United States. I rafted down the Colorado River through the Grand Canyon and have been to Colorado to go four-wheeling, elk hunting and trout fishing more times than I can count.

In 1990, I got a call from my brother Bob that change my life. He told me he had cancer. Four of my uncles had died of this disease and both my parents had battled it. My brother

Lowell and I went to Kansas for Bob's surgery. The doctor came out afterwards and told us the bad news. The cancer had spread to Bob's liver and he would have to undergo Chemo Therapy. On my way home, I tried to think about how I could help Bob. I knew the only thing I could do was to pray and ask God to heal him, so I got back into church. Over the next three years, Bob kept getting sicker and sicker. I threw myself into my work, building houses. I would often start working very early in the morning. The police drove up to my work-site one day and told me that, if I didn't keep to designated work hours posted in the city ordinance, I would be arrested.

In the early part of 1993, I awoke one morning to take a walk on my property. It was about 5:30 am and I was thinking that I couldn't feel any lower if I dug a hole and climbed down in it. As I continued to walk to the edge of my property, I was screaming at God to help my brother. Suddenly, a peace came over me, a peace I hadn't known in three years. I cried out to God, "What's happening?" Just then a thought came to me. Vickie is home praying for me. I looked at my watch; it read 6:48. I walked quickly back to the house and found Vickie sitting at the breakfast bar. I said, "You were praying for me at twelve minutes until 7:00." She started crying and said, "How did you know?" I told her I knew her prayers were answered. Maybe mine weren't, but hers were. I now knew there was a God and this knowledge kept me going for the next two years.

I was hunting on Spruce Mountain in Colorado when I decided to give Bob a call and check up on him. I asked how he was doing and he told me he would be going in for surgery to remove some more of the cancer growths. I could hardly speak when I heard the news. I assured Bob that I would be there for him. I got off the phone and sat down and cried. I returned to Missouri, got my camper and headed to Wichita, Kansas, like I promised Bob I would. The surgeon that performed the surgery told us that he took part of Bob's colon, liver and lung. I stayed with Bob's wife until 8:00 pm and then went to a hotel to sleep for a couple of hours. My sister-in-law called and asked me to come back; there was a problem with Bob. When I got to the hospital, we went to ICU, but they wouldn't let us in. We were taken back to the waiting room where a minister offered to pray for Bob. We prayed together and then I picked up a Gideon Bible and started reading everything I could about God's mercy and grace. About a half an hour later, the surgeon came in and told us Bob's heart had stopped, but they were able to bring him back. They let us go into his room where the doctor introduced us to my brother's nurse, Victor. When the doctor left, so did Victor. I was very mad that Victor wasn't paying the attention to Bob that I thought he required since they had all the equipment alarms on silent. Bob's blood pressure had dropped to 80/60 with no response from Victor. It wasn't long before it dropped even more to 60/40. Hate started to enter me when I thought to myself, *I haven't been on my knees praying for five years only to see Bob die in front of me.* I looked back at the blood pressure again and saw it even lower at 50/30 and at that point I snapped. I walked out to where Victor was reading his newspaper, looked him in the eye and said, "My brother is dying and he needs blood and needs it now!" Victor told me that he ordered it a while ago and it hadn't shown up yet. As he turned in his chair, he saw it on the desk behind him. It's a wonder I didn't kill him right there. Victor got the blood and hooked everything up quickly. Bob's pressure started back up. "We have to get the doctor back because there's a problem." I knew one problem was Victor. I wonder if it was because of him that my brother had died two hours earlier. If Bob had died in front of me, I probably would've killed Victor on the spot. We were told to go to the waiting room until the doctor could check on Bob. I stayed in there praying for about 15 minutes and then the doctor came in to talk with us. He said that Bob was bleeding and if they could find the area, they could fix it. A long 45 minutes later he came back in and said Bob would be fine. I was so relieved; I could've kissed the doctor's feet even if he had been walking through a cow pasture! Bob was released and went home ten days later. I went home and when Sunday came, I went forward and joined the church and was baptized. I knew God had been with me through the whole ordeal.

Bob lived for another 3½ years and was able to see the birth of his granddaughter who would always bring a smile to his face when she climbed up in his lap.

About two weeks after I was baptized, I started having a problem. When I was alone working, a voice from within came to me and said, "If you hadn't been there, your brother would be dead." I didn't disagree with the thought. This went on and on and kept eating at me. I couldn't release the hate I felt and it got worse over the next seven years. I was working one day in the field and God said, "Look at yourself." When I went to church on Sunday, I asked Pastor Leroy if I could speak. I told the congregation about my problem. I tried to forgive Victor for what he did and didn't do. Did I owe my salvation to Victor? Should I love him instead of hating him? The answers are yes to both. If he had done his job, I may not have gone to church, much less be baptized. I felt better when I was done speaking. Some people told me that my words had opened their eyes to the possibility that hate was bothering them, as well. One man even told me that hearing about my love for my brother was making him want to make things right between him and his brother. Thank God.

November 11, 2002, a perfect night. There was no moon, clear water and the temperature was about 40 degrees. I had already put a few fish in the boat when sadness came over me. I think it was a hate cloud. I started to sob and asked my friend to pull the boat to the bank. I got out of the boat and sat down on the gravel bar and cried my eyes out. My friend asked if I was sick and I told him my problem; a demon was in me. I said, "Vickie is home praying for me, Pastor Leroy is praying for me and my church is praying for me." I thought I was through with my hate for Victor when I forgave him. My friend grabbed me by my arm and told me if I didn't get rid of the hate, it would surely kill me. Seven years is too long to have such a thing eating at you. He told me he would pray that it would leave me. I felt better after talking to him and went back to the cabin to sleep. In the middle of the night, a voice woke me. It said, "Kenneth, you know how you felt when they cut into your brother; now you know how I felt when they drove the nails into Jesus' hands." I realized that God Almighty was speaking to me and at that instant; I knew that God did love me. I knew Vickie was right, Leroy was right and the book of John was right. God is love (John 3:16). I knew God would not speak to me if He didn't love me. The tears started flowing down my cheeks and soaking my pillow. Before this night, I would tell my wife that I was no good and that I didn't know what the word "love" meant. It sure wasn't hard to love my neighbor more than myself because I didn't love myself.

As soon as the voice stopped, I had a vision of myself lying in slime. I was crawling around on my belly, trying to get out. As I was struggling, I looked to the right. The bank was steep and there was nothing to hold on to. I looked to the left and saw the same thing. There was so much slime in my eyes, I could hardly see. I looked ahead of me and saw a clean white rock about five or six feet away. The bank was too steep and there were no branches to pull myself up. I wanted out of the slime; I wanted up on that clean white rock. I noticed someone standing on the rock and I started screaming. "There's someone on the rock!" It was Jesus. He reached down and pulled me up on the rock with Him. I was standing on this beautiful clean white rock with my Lord and Savior, Jesus Christ.

As I looked at Him, I noticed He was taller than me and I couldn't see His face. As I looked down at His arm, I saw a line between His hand and elbow. I guess the line showed me how far down He had to reach to pull me up out of the slime and sin of this world. He didn't say that I was too dirty to touch. There was no dirt on Jesus. He appeared to have a white glow around Him. As I looked down at His feet and the white rock we were standing on, I saw my own feet. I couldn't believe my eyes. As I started to focus on my legs, waist, chest and arms, I didn't have any dirt or slime on me at all. When He touched me, He cleansed me. Tears of joy were flowing down my face. Just off to the right, I saw what Jesus had pulled me out of. I began saying over and over, "That's the sin of the world." With tears still running down my face, I saw blue sky and felt wonderful joy. The light was like looking at a sky without any clouds. It then turned from blue to a bright light. It was so bright I thought my eyes should be hurting, but they weren't.

The joy I felt just can't be described. In front of the light there were gold-colored bars that kept getting shorter the further I looked to the left. It was like standing and looking down a fence row. To the right was nothing but gray. As I looked back at the light, I started saying, "That's Heaven! That's Heaven! I know the joy of Heaven! I'm looking into Heaven." God was letting me look into Heaven. Then I looked back at the gray and I asked, "Where's the gate?" I wanted in. The next instance, I was fully awake and the light I was seeing was daylight. I jumped up and sat on the edge of the bed and started shouting. "I've got to tell someone! I've got to tell someone about this wonderful thing that's just happened to me. I'll tell my mother in the next room; no, she is 87 and she wouldn't understand why I was waking her up so early. I've got to tell Vickie," I thought, *she'll understand.*

I grabbed my cell phone and looked at it. No signal! I had to go up the hill to get service. I put the phone in my pocket and ran out the door of the cabin. When the cold air hit my face, I knew one thing; I didn't hate anyone. Hate didn't mean anything to me. I ran up the hill and didn't feel any pain. I was 66 years old, had arthritis, gout and Addison's disease and I wasn't even out of breath. I saw two piles of clean, white rock. I ran to the top of the first pile and started shouting, "I am free! I am free! I am free!" I ran down that pile and up the other and yelled again, "I'm free!" I stopped as I came to my senses and knew I would wake the dogs on the farm a quarter mile away. I pulled out the cell phone and called Vickie. A sleepy voice answered and I shouted, "It's payback time!" She said, "What do you mean?" I replied, "You have been on your knees praying for me for 45 years and today is your day. It's your payday." She pleaded with me to tell her what I meant. I said, "I'll tell you what I mean…God spoke to me. Jesus pulled me up out of the sin of the world and stood me on a rock with Him. I looked into Heaven." All I heard at the other end was crying. I told her if I got killed on I-44 on my way home today not to cry because I will be in a better place.

When I went home after God called my name, I stopped and told my friend Ken what had happened. I went to church and told Pastor Leroy my testimony. He didn't even know me; I was changed. When he heard my story, he said, "You will have to go to other churches and tell what God did for you." I didn't know whether I could do that or not. He said, "You will be able to because you've got the Holy Spirit with you." I can now sing specials in church, talk to a crowd of people without fear and speak to strangers on the street. I do not have hate in me anymore. Praise God! I know now why God showed me what He did. He wants me to tell everyone what I've seen and that He has work for me to do. I have a new job and a new business card. It reads: GOD SPOKE

TO ME / WILLING TO SHARE MY TESTIMONY / ANY TIME, ANY PLACE.

After I saw the light of Heaven, was pulled out of the slime pit of Hell, and heard God's voice, I was a different person. I was changed. I slowed down on building houses and started doing more church work. I went to hospitals to check on and pray for church members. During the next year, I was a guest speaker at more than twenty-six churches. In the next five years, my life had completely changed. When I tell people how God changed me and they don't want to hear it, when they reject the Word of God, they almost sign their own death warrant. I know if they don't change, they will die and go to Hell.

TESTIMONIES

I started going to visit other churches to give my testimony and often people would share theirs as well. Some people would say, "I've never told anyone this." After hearing them, I couldn't understand how they could keep it to themselves.

Some of the following are testimonies people have shared with me and some are my own. Each one indicates how our Heavenly Father is working in our lives. Some are with His healing hand, some with His encouragement and others with miracles of the Holy Spirit.

Throughout the following testimonies you'll find some names mentioned several times. Here is a brief introduction to those people.

Vickie (Campbell) is my wife. We've been married for over 51 years.

Pastor Leroy (Nixon) has been the pastor at Second Baptist Church for 10 years.

Ken (Jones) is one of my best friends and a partner in my travels.

ON LIGHT

❧

"Then spake Jesus again unto them, saying, I am the light of the world; he that followeth me shall not walk in darkness, but shall have the light of life." John 8:12

✳ A man told me he saw the light right after he came up out of the water when he was baptized. When he came to his senses, people were shaking him because they thought something was wrong with him. He made the comment, "It was so wonderful and I wish they would have left me alone."

*A lady said that she saw the light and her comment was, "It was glorious."

*Caroline said she saw the light after the birth of her baby. The doctors couldn't get the bleeding to stop and she thought she was dying. When a wonderful light came upon her, she said she had a nice feeling and such peace. She didn't have any bad feelings nor was she scared of dying.

*One woman said she died and the doctors brought her back twice. She saw a glorious light, had a feeling of peace and no fear.

*A 72-year-old man fell out of his chair and died. His wife gave him C.P.R and managed to bring him back. While he was out, he saw a light through a tunnel. He told me that, at that time, he didn't care whether he came back or not. Since then he started going to church, accepted the Lord and was baptized. Praise God!

*Another woman shared with me that she was in the hospital when her heart stopped. She saw a light at the end of a tunnel and started to move towards it. Although the light was incredibly bright, it didn't hurt her eyes. Then she saw Jesus in the light. She wasn't scared at all and felt at peace. The doctor gave her a shot directly in her heart and brought her back.

*While in a store, I shared my testimony with a woman. She then told me about the time she was admitted to the hospital for surgery. As they wheeled her down the hall on the gurney, she felt a bright light come upon her. It stayed on her in the elevator and all the subsequent turns to the operating room. Later, in the recovery room, she told her kids what had happened. They told her that it was just the normal lights of the hospital. They finally put her in a wheel-chair to retrace the route she took to the operating room. She told them that the lights were not nearly as bright nor as wonderful as the ones she saw.

*Charlie has a disease and was hospitalized. While there, his heart stopped. He saw a bright light upon him and thought he saw small angels sitting on his chest. Then he felt them hitting him on his sides. He said, "I guess it was those paddles they use to get your heart beating again."

*A preacher's wife, named Barbara, came up to me after I gave my testimony at a revival meeting. She was crying for joy after hearing about me seeing the wonderful light of Heaven. She, too, had seen the light and in it was a mansion. She was only able to see the outside of this mansion. During a visit to Florida, Barbara's friend told her that she had seen the light of Heaven and a mansion. She only saw the inside. The two women thought they had seen the same mansion.

31

One had seen the inside; the other had seen the outside. She also knew four other people who have seen the light.

*During a revival at church, a man mentioned that he was in a car accident when he was nine years old and was told that he was dead for a while. He said that a bright light had appeared and in it he saw a gate. Although he tried, he could not open the gate.

*While on a cruise to Alaska with Charles Stanley in 2004, we were given these testimonies:

I started talking to a man named Quigley in the ship's swimming pool. I gave him my testimony. He said he had a similar experience. He didn't tell me the details, but he did say that when he went to bed one night he was one person, and when he got up the next day, he was entirely different. He said that his friends don't really know him anymore.

As we came up the steps of the ship one day, I almost ran into this lady who was about 40 or 50 years old. She looked upset and I started talking to her. I told her my testimony about how God set me free and how I didn't have hate for anyone or anything. As I was talking to her, Quigley walked up and joined us and agreed with me. Now the four of us were at the top of the stairs. The lady seemed to calm down and asked me if we would like to hear her testimony. She said she had a daughter who was 20 years old when she was killed in a car crash. The man who hit her daughter didn't have a scratch. I asked if her daughter was a Christian, and she said yes. She said she got mad at God. She had a heart problem, went to the hospital with a heart attack and died. They brought her back to life. While she was gone, she saw a wonderful light, and now knows what joy her daughter is in. She said that she started thinking about the man who hit her daughter. She knew he was not a Christian. As she was recovering, she reasoned with herself that the man was given a chance to get right with God.

The next day, we were in a building that covered about two acres. The entire luggage from the ship was stacked around on the floor. Our luggage was within ten feet from the lady we had talked with us before. We started talking again, and she had another testimony to give. She said she was a nurse in a large hospital. She works in a unit that deals with people who are dying. She said there is a big difference between the people who know the Lord and the ones who do not. The Christians seem at peace when they die. The non-Christians will often ask her to put cold water on their feet because they are so hot. I feel they may be feeling the fires of Hell already. I try to tell these people about God and they just won't listen. It makes me feel so bad.

We sent Quigley a tape of my testimony. He wrote back and said he goes to meetings and shares his testimony. He then shows my tape. God works wonders in people if you are just willing to share. Give and it shall be given back to you many times over. (Luke 6:38)

GOD CALLED

"…Then said I, Here Am I Send Me." Isaiah 6:8

﹡Two deacons had the job of interviewing two men for Pastor of their church. Both applicants were well qualified and neither deacon could make up his mind. For the next month, they prayed about it, but still couldn't seem to decide. Then in the middle of the night, one was scared by a voice calling out, "Paul." He got up early in the morning, called the other deacon and said, "We are going to hire Paul." Thirteen years later, Paul is still with the same church and they are expanding. The deacon that hired Paul says, "If you tell some people that you heard a voice in the night, they think you're weird. Paul was not the man that I was working with."

*A man was driving a concrete truck on the way to Fort Leonard Wood and heard God call his name. It scared him so badly that he jammed on the brakes. God told him to go to his ex-wife and tell her that if she didn't come back to him and their little girl, God would strip her of all her blessings. The driver said that he couldn't do that. He then heard God say, "That's what I want." The driver did what God had told him, but his ex-wife didn't want to hear about it and hasn't come back yet.

*My friend Bryan tells of when God called out to him. "I was starting a 4½-hour drive to Kansas City to drop off a bid for work. It was a beautiful October day, perfect for a relaxing drive. Suddenly I felt a slight pain in my left side. I pulled off at a gas station and bought a soda and some aspirin, which I took immediately. After a few minutes, I decided that it was nothing and pulled back onto the highway. I had only gone about four more miles when another pain hit and I felt flushed from head to toe. I pulled over again, but this time called my brother on my cell phone to tell him something was wrong. I gave him my location and told him to call an ambulance. While I waited for help, I found a piece of paper and a pen and started writing a note to my three kids telling them of my love for them. When my peripheral vision started to darken, I started writing faster. I then wrote a list of things I wished I'd done. Fifth on my list was that I wished I could've done more for God. I felt like I was slipping into a dark abyss and it had become difficult to breath. Just then I heard an inaudible voice that said, 'Bryan, why am I so far down on your list?' In that moment, I felt shame and remorse and I told God that I was sorry. My vision slowly started to clear again and after being taken to the hospital, I underwent a triple by-pass. I believe that sometimes God puts you flat on your back so that you can look straight up."

*Tommy, a preacher from Texas, gave me a testimony of how he was driving a truck for a company in the Kansas City area. He went around a corner and saw a building on his right. He felt the Holy Spirit come upon him and he felt strongly that he should preach in that building. He located the owner and negotiated rent for the building. He put up a sign and announced that he would be preaching a service there and gave the time and date.

When that day came, he arrived an hour early to greet the people that would come. After waiting more than 45 minutes and no one showing up he asked, "God, what do you want me to do?" He was told to set up 25 chairs in a circle. Still no one showed up. He again asked, "God, what do you want me to do?" God impressed upon him to preach and so he did. For 45 minutes he preached to 25 empty chairs. When he was done, with sweat dripping off of him, he folded up the chairs and locked the door. As he was leaving, some people showed up and he informed them that the service was over. A year later, when he was asked to preach at another church, they requested a picture of him. They put his picture on a billboard beside the highway coming into town so anyone traveling through would see it. When the evening to preach came, a man approached him and handed him a check for $1000 and with it the strangest story he ever heard. The man said that about a year earlier he was in an empty building and a guy set up 25 chairs in a circle and started preaching. The man hid behind a piano and listened to the sermon. About halfway through it, the Holy Spirit came upon him and he accepted the Lord as his Savior right there behind the piano. The man said he would've liked to stay to hear Tommy preach, but he too was a preacher now and was needed out of town. He just wanted to drop off the check as an offering.

ANGELS

"Behold, I send an angel before thee, to keep thee in the way, and to bring thee into the place which I have prepared." Exodus 23:20

✶ A preacher said he was diving in a lake with scuba gear on and lost his facemask. The weights on his legs were pulling him to the bottom and he knew he would drown. He found a rope on the bottom of the lake and tried to pull himself out with it. He had gone only a few yards when he fell to his knees and saw a bright light. It was so bright he couldn't even look towards it. The man cried out to the Lord, "I thought you wanted me to take care of my wife and train my kids." As he fell, he hit his head on a concrete pier under the water. The next thing he knew, he was on top of the pier and three feet above the water. He was very sick, but alive. He told me he wouldn't have had the strength to climb the pier. When I asked him how he got out, he said he believes that we all have angels who watch over us. This is the only explanation he could give.

*A lady I know has a girlfriend who was going through a terrible divorce. Her ex-husband would often drive to her house and come up in the driveway. Because of his previous threats, this woman was quite scared of him. She asked my friend to pray for her and that her ex-husband would stay away from the property. As the lady prayed for her girl-friend, she had a vision. She saw two white figures standing like guards with large lances in their hands at either side of her girlfriend's driveway. Sometime later, my friend saw this woman again and was told that the ex-husband had not been back. She said it was almost like there was an invisible fence blocking the driveway.

*Another lady told me of the time she went in to the hospital to have surgery to repair the hole she had in her heart since childhood. She told me, the night prior to the surgery, she saw someone sitting in a chair in a dark corner of her room. She didn't know if it was an angel or Jesus, but it gave her a good feeling. She has recovered and is doing well.

*While making my rounds at the hospital recently, I came across a man I hadn't seen in a very long time. As children, we swam in the same swimming hole at the creek near where we both lived. More than fifty years have passed since then. I gave him my testimony and he volunteered a personal experience that had influenced his life. When he was nine years old, he and his Mom moved to New Mexico. They lived, for several years, in a bad neighborhood. While walking home one night, three boys grabbed him and threw him into a deep pit. He remembered falling, but did not hit the bottom. He felt himself being lifted and carried up to the ledge at the opposite side of the pit. "Before I could go very far, I heard them at the edge of the pit calling for me. They apparently could not see me." He had not one mark on him, wasn't dirty or hurt and arrived home safely. When I asked him what had saved him, he confided in me that his Grandmother was always praying for his safety. He believes that a guardian angel appeared when he had the need. He believes that we all have a guardian angel watching over us. Since then, he has had other things happen to him that he can't explain. Once, this same man was in church listening to a Singer perform. The singer searched him out afterwards and told him that he saw an angel standing behind him during the whole performance.

*Alone on a cold winter day, a woman was debating on whether to take a gravel road to her mother's house. Her husband had taken the children over there earlier in the day and the woman had warned him not to take that gravel road, fearing that ice may be on it. Now as she looked at that same road, it didn't look that bad and besides, it would save her travel time. She hadn't gone very far when she realized that she had made a mistake. The north side of the steep hill was completely iced. The car stopped about halfway up the hill. She got out of the car to put something under the tires, even though she is handicapped with a brace that she has worn since she had polio as a child. She started praying that God would help her. When she looked up, she saw four huge white figures standing by her car. She was scared, but tried again to drive the car forward. The car began to slip towards a ditch, but she put it in reverse and was able to back down the hill to a flat area without leaving the road. Once again, she called out for help from Heaven, put the car in drive and went up the hill like it wasn't even there. She didn't see any wings on the white figures, but felt like they were angels put there to protect her. As she told me, "Something had to keep the car from sliding into that ditch."

*One woman told me of a time when she was a teenager and was returning from church, she saw a large figure in a white robe down by the family chicken house. Although she saw no face, she felt that it was either Jesus or a guardian angel. She has been near death several times since then.

*An elderly man at a nursing home told me of how God saved him while in the Army in Vietnam. He and several other soldiers were ordered to drive a Jeep through a pass monitored by the enemy. They were told that it was likely that they would come under fire. Doing what they were told, they took off towards the pass. As they topped a hill, the enemy began shooting and bullets were hitting the Jeep from every direction. They drove as fast as they could until they were out of range. When the soldiers got out to assess the damage, they couldn't lay a hand on any part of the Jeep that wasn't bullet ridden. They were shocked to see that no tires, gas lines or wires had been hit, nor were any of the passengers even scratched. They knew that God or His angels had been with them protecting them.

*While on a cruise ship with other Christians, I spoke with two gentlemen from old Mexico who shared stories of their time in Vietnam. One told me a story that was the same as the one you just read from the man in the nursing home and I wondered if they had been in the same Jeep. The second man told me that he took care of airplanes. He said one day a plane came in and landed and he could tell something was wrong. As the passengers came out one by one they stared back at the plane. It had bullet holes everywhere and when counted, they numbered four hundred. Again, no tires, gas lines or wires had been hit, nor were any of the passengers hurt. I personally think that these men were fighting for the rights of other people and God blessed them with His love and compassion.

*I was working on the roof of a house we were tearing down for a church parking lot. One day when Ed drove up. He got out of his car and came towards the church and said, "Where did Clayton go?" I told Ed that Clayton wasn't here yet. He said, "I just saw him standing up there next to you." I joked that Ed must have been drinking, but he insisted that he saw someone up on the roof with me. Just then, the chimney fell and barely missed my head. Although I had a few cuts on my arms, I was not hurt. I was thankful it wasn't worse. Maybe it was an angel that Ed saw up on that roof with me. Later he gave this testimony at church on a Sunday morning.

When we got the basement poured for the church I was there alone working one day. I went up the hill on the east side and was standing between the old church and the new basement. I slipped and started to fall into the backfill, heading south. I fell, but the next thing I knew I was facing north on the same bank I had fallen from. There is no way I could have spun around and landed on the same bank. Maybe Ed was right again; an angel had saved me. It was all in God's plan.

*My ministry has taken me into hospitals and nursing homes. I called on a man named Jim. He said his brother got sick and wanted to know if I could have my pastor come out and see him. My pastor went to see him. "My brother had never asked Jesus to come into his life." He told the pastor that he wanted him to help him before it was too late. The pastor helped lead him to Christ through the Holy Spirit, who is the only one that can convict of sin. About 2 weeks later Jim said, "I got a call from my brother that I needed to see him right away. When I got there he was in bed. He said, 'I am sure glad to see you. Jim, there are angels all around my bed waiting to take me to heaven.'" Jim said he put his arms up in the air and died. Praise God, I know where he is.

*Lola and Henry were traveling down a highway in their car, singing praises to the Lord. They met a patrolman that they knew and he was pointing to them. They went on their journey and stopped at a store in a small town. They met another patrolman and thought he was going to hit them. They looked out the windshield and saw wings of an angel over their car. They talked to both patrolman and the patrolman said they both saw the angel protecting them.

*I met a lady that told me of a time when she, a single mom, was traveling from New Mexico to Missouri with four small children. They were headed home. It started snowing on their journey and they did not have any warm clothes. They were traveling by bus and while at a bus station stop, the children were fussing because they were hungry. The lady was out of money and couldn't buy any food. A man approached her and offered to buy the children something to eat. The lady refused, saying that she did not accept charity. He approached her a little later and she again refused and said, "No thank you; we will be fine" even though she was also getting hungry. He came by a third time and threw a $20.00 bill on the table and walked out the door. She said, "I jumped up and went out the door to thank him and I couldn't find him anywhere. I think he was an angel sent to help me in my time of need."

VISIONS

*"And it shall come to pass in the last days, saith
God, I will pour out of my Spirit upon all flesh;
and your sons and your daughters shall prophesy,
and your young men shall see visions, and your
old men shall dream dreams:" Acts 2:17*

* A man I've known for over 40 years shared something he had never told anyone before. While at a
tent revival as a teen, he saw a halo form over the preacher's
head while he was preaching. My friend didn't ask anyone
else if they saw it, but he knows he did.

*A Church of Christ member told me that she is afraid of
water and had a dream that she was going across the Jordan
River. She noticed that it was muddy. About halfway across,
a hand with scars on the back reached out to her. She held it
until she reached the other side of the river.

*I've known my friend Larry for over 40 years. He was
blind and now needed an operation on his leg. While in the
hospital, he had a heart attack due to a blood clot and my
friend passed away five days later. I was with him when he
left this earth. Two days before his funeral service, I had a
dream or vision of Larry. I saw him walking with a big smile
on his face. He was not blind nor using a cane. I called his

mother and told her what I had seen. She started crying with joy. She knew he was no longer in pain. Praise God.

*Sometimes I dream about things and then I see them the next day. My friend Ken and I were in Colorado, up by Spruce Mountain. We were spending time riding the 4-wheeler and fishing for small trout. On Sunday, we would go to church in town and tell people what Jesus has done for both of us. One night, I had a dream that I saw a cattle guard that was made of white canvas with black stripes on it. Once it was staked down, the cattle wouldn't cross it. The next morning we woke and headed south from our camp spot. We had only traveled about two miles when we came upon a cattle guard made of white canvas with black stripes. When we got on the other side of it, I stopped and said to Ken, "I saw this in a dream I had last night." I don't know if this was a message from God, or what it meant.

*It says, in the scripture, that old men will dream dreams. I have started seeing things before they happen; call them dreams or visions. I had one about a young man at our church very early one Sunday morning. I saw him at about two or three years older than he is now and doing something he should not be doing. Later that morning while at church, I saw this same young man doing what I had seen him do in my vision. Not wanting to stir up trouble at church, I waited until that evening to tell my wife. She too was shocked. The next day, I spoke with one of our Pastors and told him of my vision and what I witnessed at church. He could hardly wait for me to finish telling him because a woman had approached him after the service and told him what she had seen the young man doing. She had told the Pastor the same story I had just shared with him. All I can say is that it puts a load on me to think that God is doing this in my life.

*Larry Eaten gave me a testimony that his brother-in-law related to him. Over 20 years ago his brother-in-law was driving down the road and had a brain aneurysm. He ended up in a Nashville hospital. While he was there, he had this dream or vision. He was climbing a ladder and Satan was on the other side climbing with him. As he was climbing, Satan was trying to pry his fingers off the ladder. When he finally got to the top, Jesus was there and picked him up and carried him across some rough water. He said Jesus' face was shining like the sun. It was as if he could read his mind. There was a conversation, but no actual words were spoken. Jesus told him that it wasn't as hard to get to heaven as people think it is. Larry said when he looked off in the distance, he could see the outline of a city with mansions. He saw grass and flowers so beautiful he couldn't explain them. There was a path in the grass and he saw his mother coming toward him. She was motioning for him to come on home. Her face was glowing just like Jesus' was. His mother had been dead for over 20 years. He could look back to earth and see through walls. He saw his wife and kids home crying. He asked the Lord if he could go back because his family needed him. The next thing he knew he was back in the hospital and in pain.

*My wife Vickie and I went to a week's worth of classes called *Evangelistic Explosion* to learn how to witness to people in their homes and to bring them to a saving knowledge of Jesus. I got to class early one morning and told the instructor, a Baptist preacher, a testimony about friends. I said that if you have a friend, you will try to tell him about the plan of salvation. When the class started, the first thing the instructor said was that we were going to talk about friends that morning. When break time came, I went up and asked the instructor if he chose the subject of friends because of what I had said. As he smiled at me, he shared that it was already what he had written in his notes.

*Two months prior to attending the *Evangelistic Explosion,* I had a dream and shared it with my wife Vickie. I told her I thought I knew what was on the other side of the fence around Heaven. I saw red hills that were high on the left and then dropped off to the right. The valley was covered with a red fog, kind of like the hills in Missouri during the fall. I didn't think much about it again until one day, while attending this seminar, we were shown a presentation with pictures and music. One of the pictures was the exact sight I had seen in my vision. Tears filled my eyes and I turned to look at Vickie. What an awesome God we serve.

*The name Joe came to me in a vision as I saw an obituary in the paper. I know a "Joe" who lives about twenty miles from me, so I tried to call him. When I didn't get an answer, Vickie and I drove to his farm to check on him. When he answered the door, we knew that he was ill. With a smile on his face, he said that he had Hodgkin's and with chemotherapy, it was easily treatable. I asked if he went to church and he revealed he hadn't gone since he was a child. I told him how I was changed through the power of God and then finished our visit. I called him two weeks later. He said he was doing fine, but was not able to talk right then. I thought I would hear from him, but I haven't. I asked one of his neighbors if he had seen Joe lately. They had and said he didn't look very good. Best I can tell, if he died today, he would not go to Heaven.

*The name Bob came to me in a vision and I knew who it was. I got up and told Vickie I felt that I had to call him. I couldn't find Bob, but found a former co-worker that had his number. I tried several times to reach him and left messages every time, but Bob never returned my call. I talked to God and told Him I did my best to reach out to Bob, and now I'm through calling him. About a month later, Vickie and I were walking around at an outdoor arts and crafts festival. We turned a corner and virtually ran into Bob. When asked why he never returned the phone calls, he replied that he was in such pain he didn't want to talk to anyone. At that point, I knew that God was working. We talked for about 30 minutes and he told Vickie and me that he was envious of us because we truly believed in God. I invited him to our home to talk more, but he never showed up. About a month later, Vickie and I had just sat down at a café in town for lunch. I said, "God is working." When she asked what I meant, I pointed to Bob sitting behind her in a corner booth. I ate quickly and then invited myself to sit down with Bob. Again we talked for about 30 minutes and then left with the promise of a phone call soon. Another month went by and I ran into Bob in town again. He said that he was heading east to stay with his parents for a while. He said he still had my card and would call soon. It's been four months and I still haven't heard from Bob. I feel that God kept putting him in front of me with hope that he would reach out. I hope he gets right with God before it's too late.

   *I had a dream or vision while at our river cabin. In it, a man's face appeared to me. I knew him, but I couldn't put a name to the face. Then I finally figured out who he was. The word "drunk" came to me. This was strange because I never knew that he drank. Then I saw this parking lot and he was going up the hill on a diagonal toward a white car sitting at the top. He wasn't staggering. He was walking in a straight line. The car had the dome light on and it looked like there were two or three people in it. There was a woman standing about 20 or 30 ft behind the car, in a small street or ally. He went over by the woman. When he got close to her, she struck him in the head with something. It almost knocked him down. He left her and staggered off down a hill by a building. I didn't see the building, but I know there was one there. I thought he might be hurt so I ran around the building to head him off or to see if I could help him. I went around behind the building, but I couldn't find him. I went back to the parking lot. The white car had moved down and was headed into the building. There were two strong boys that were picking up on the back bumper and swaying the car back and forth. I walked over to the car and opened the right passenger door and bent over and looked in. There was a big guy sitting in the seat with the dome light on. I didn't bend down enough to see his face. I walked back up the hill where I first saw the woman. She was gone. I looked down and there lay a brown beer bottle in the street. In all this vision, I had the feeling that she loved him. The boys loved him too. There was no hate.

I got up the next morning at 5 a.m. and started writing all this down while it was fresh in my mind. I tried to lie back down and get a little sleep, but I couldn't. There was such an urgency I felt. I just had to go out and find this guy. I drove the 35 miles home and surprised my wife because she thought I was going to cut wood for the house that day.

I waited until 8 a.m. and started to call different people. I had not seen this man for at least three or maybe even six months. I finally found someone that had his cell phone number. He was 35 miles east from my home. I said I would drive over and talk to him. He said he was coming back to Rolla and he would stop at my house about 2:30 p.m.

Needless to say, I was nervous. I thought of all the things this might mean. One thing I thought it might mean, when he was going down the hill, was that he was going to Hell, or was he going to hurt himself? Then I kept thinking about the love I felt in this dream or vision. When I told him about the dream or vision he said he didn't drink, but his wife drinks beer. When I told him about the two strong men, he said he had two strong boys. He also said he drove a white car. I know when I looked in the white car there was a large man sitting in the seat. I did not see his face, but he was big like the man in the dream or vision. This man confided in me that one time his mother-in-law was in a hospital. He told his wife something about her. When his wife came home, she said that her mother told her the same thing, to the very word what he had said. I think that there is some trouble in this family. It might pertain to her drinking beer.

OUT OF BODY

"And I knew such a man, (whether in the body, or out of the body, I cannot tell: God knoweth;)
2 Corinthians 12:3

✳ A preacher was at a hospital with his wife when his heart stopped. She was able to perform C.P.R. and get his heart beating again. When he came to, he said that his soul had come out of his body and had risen up towards the ceiling and then returned when she brought him back. He said he watched her giving him C.P.R. The preacher said this proves to him that our soul comes out of our body when we die.

*A young man got a call from his mother saying that his Dad had fallen in the hallway and she thought he might be dead. He told his mother, "Dad will be alright." The young man rushed over and found his mother and dad in the hall. She was trying to get her husband breathing again and together they brought him back. Later, the father revealed that his soul had come out of his body and floated up to the ceiling. He had watched them trying to help him and then his soul went back down into his body.

*A visitor came to church one Sunday and after hearing my testimony, he wanted to share his. He told of a time many years ago when he was working on a construction crew putting up towers. His boss approached him around quitting time and said he needed to show him something up on the tower. Since it would be for just a few minutes, they didn't bother with the safety harness. They were up around thirty feet when the wind blew him off the scaffold. As a trained paratrooper, he automatically curled into a tuck position, but broke both legs upon landing and was knocked out. When he came to, he said his feet were on backwards. He told one of his guys to jerk his legs out straight. The guy said, "I can't do that." He replied, "As long as you work for me, you will do what I say." When the guy did as he wad told, the injured man thinks he died. The next thing he knew, he was walking around and saw all these people working on someone. "When I got closer, I saw it was me." They brought him back to life and his soul went back into his body. After being loaded into an ambulance, he died two more times on the way to the hospital. Both times he said he felt like he was going through the floor. While in the hospital, the doctor informed him that he would never walk again. He informed the doctor that he had a God who can fix anything. The doctor said if physical therapy couldn't have him walking within four months, he would never be able to do it. Four months came and went without much improvement, but at five months he was able to take a few steps. I don't know how long it took, but at the time of his visit to our church, you would never have known that anything had been wrong. His doctor told him that his recovery was a miracle and they still talk almost every day. His doctor now believes in God and has accepted Jesus Christ.

MIRACLES

"God also bearing them witness, both with signs and wonders, and with divers miracles, and gifts of the Holy Ghost, according to his own will."
Hebrews 2:4

✱ A preacher had a serious illness that put him in the hospital about two times a year. He was getting sick late one evening and told his wife that he could make it through the night, but would need to go to the hospital the next day. In the middle of the night, he heard a voice say, "It's 3:00 a.m. and you're healed." The preacher looked at the clock and it read 3:00 a.m. He started to poke and press on his chest and belly where he normally felt pain and there was none. He has never needed to go to the hospital since and is doing well.

*Smokers had always bothered a woman I met until the day two of them saved her husband's life. He was having a heart attack and she drove him to the hospital. Before she could even call for help, two men smoking outside the hospital doors rushed over and started C.P.R. and saved him. She used to get upset about people smoking, but this time it was for the best.

*A 91-year-old preacher is a walking miracle. He had a brain tumor and his doctors didn't give him any hope for recovery. They said even if they surgically removed the tumor, that it would just grow back. The man insisted on the operation anyway. They removed the tumor without any bad effects from the surgery and it has not grown back. The doctors agreed that it was a miracle.

*The mother of a soldier serving in Iraq came to our church and asked for prayer for her son's safety. She said she was going to all the churches in town asking for prayer. I never saw her again until one afternoon. Vickie and I were going door to door inviting people to our church and happened to find her. When we realized that she was the same woman who had asked for prayer for her son, we asked how he was doing. She showed us a picture of what looked like a pile of scrap metal. It was a helicopter that her son and thirteen other soldiers were on when it crashed. Her son was the only one to walk away from it without injury. Thank you, God, for protecting this young man.

*When God called my name and turned my life around, I became a changed person. God has been blessing me with a gift. One Sunday as I entered the church, I started talking to the pastor. I said, "You are going to preach on John 14?" He asked how I could possibly know that. I said, "Are you?" and with a shocked expression he said yes. The next Sunday morning I was taking a shower and started singing. I never sing in the shower. When I got out, my wife Vickie, who is the music director, said that she didn't even know that I knew that song and it happened to be the invitation song for that day.

*Vickie and I like to take our camper to Colorado and go 4-wheeling and fishing. One year, we decided to go up on Spruce Mountain on a Sunday and take our Bible to worship God and look out over His beautiful creation. Before we left camp, we got on our knees and asked God to let us give a testimony or lift someone up with our testimony, this glorious day. We went off the main road up to about 10,200 feet in elevation, a one-and-a-half hour trip. We got on our knees and thanked God for bringing us back one more time to this beautiful spot. As we got up and turned around, we saw a young man standing behind us. He was an archery hunter and had just shot a 6 x 6 bull. I asked where he was from and if he went to church. He told us he was from Ozark, Missouri and attended the Assembly of God Church. I asked if he wanted to hear my testimony and he said yes. When I finished, he shared his with us. He had been working on a scaffold 26 feet high and fell and broke his neck lengthwise. He was in traction for 6 months. They gave him calcium shots for six months and he was able to recover. He said if God hadn't been there with him, he didn't think he would've made it. Praise God.

*In 1985, Ken Jones was working for the Missouri Highway Patrol weighing trucks. One day, he was under a truck putting scales in place when the truck driver let off the clutch and the wheels ran up on Ken's leg. If his co-worker hadn't acted quickly and pulled him out, he would be dead. He was taken to the hospital and was there several days when a doctor noticed a mole on his neck. It was suggested that he have it tested for cancer and he agreed. Sure enough, it was a stage 5 melanoma. After surgery to remove the mole and glands from under his arms, the doctor authorized his release. He had no chemo and no radiation. They told him that if he had not been run over by that truck, he probably wouldn't have had the mole checked out and would've been dead in sixty days. After the accident, Ken and his wife went to church. As they were leaving, something came over him and he told the pastor and his wife he couldn't leave. They went back into the church where he accepted Jesus Christ as his Savior. He was about 50 years old at the time. It took him three years to get back to walking normal.

*Leroy was in the hospital for a procedure on his heart. After about an hour in surgery, his doctor came out to give us an update. "We can't figure out how his heart got so strong in just one day." Ken's response to this: "I'm just an old hillbilly from Missouri and I have the answer. The power of prayer, through the power of God." No one said Amen. He went home the next day.

*Tommy was traveling with a group of Christian motorcycle riders, when one fellow pulled off to the side of the highway. Tommy, of course, followed and asked if there was a problem. The other rider told him his dash was loose and he couldn't keep running with it in that condition. Tommy asked what the rider would need to fix it and was told a 3/16 fine thread nut. After looking in their bags, they failed to find such a nut. Just then a truck pulled over and skidded to a stop, dusting them with a cloud of dirt. He asked if they needed help and they told him they needed a 3/16 fine thread nut. The truck driver reached into his pocket and pulled out the exact size nut they needed. The driver jumped back in his truck and went on down the road. It seemed that God had put him there at just the right time. Was this an angel in overalls? Do angels wear overalls?

*I had worked for Leo, as a teen, in his small corner store; he was now 92 years old. When my wife told me he had been taken to the hospital in St. Louis for extensive tests, I set out at once to be with him and his family. Vickie called the prayer chain and got it started. I arrived at about 3:00 in the afternoon and spoke to his wife Opal and friend Connie. They told me he was brought to St. Louis after a test in Rolla, MO had shown something very wrong. After we prayed together, Opal suggested that I head out for the 2-hour drive home before it got too late. She said she would call me when they got the results. I started heading for home and as I got on I-44, I thought to myself, "I'm too old to be in all this traffic. I don't want to come back here anymore." I arrived home and pulled into the garage just as my cell phone rang. It was Opal telling me that the last test was not good and that the doctors would be putting a catheter up his leg to his heart to see what was wrong. The procedure was scheduled for 9:30 a.m. the next morning. I asked if she wanted me to come back. She said she would hate for me to drive all that way. When I rephrased my question to, "Will you feel better if I'm there?" She said yes. I told her I would be back at 8:30 a.m. and I was. They took Leo down a few minutes after I arrived and Opal, Connie and I headed to the waiting room. A little while later the doctor walked up to us and said that they couldn't find anything seriously wrong. They knew he had suffered a heart attack and had proof from the test run in Rolla, but they couldn't see anything else wrong that couldn't be helped or fixed with medication. I shouted "Praise God"; no one said Amen. Leo went home the next day…Praise God.

*Vickie and I had been going door to door trying to get people to come to our church. This particular day, however, our goal was to specifically reach out to the kids who had just attended our Vacation Bible School and ask them to start coming to our Sunday school. We had already tried to reach out to several of them to no avail. Before we got in the car to start towards town, I thought to myself that we might as well stay home because most of the ones we had talked to didn't want to hear what we had to say. I repented for this thought and got in my car to try anyway. To my dismay, no one was at home at any of the places we stopped. As we were about to give up and go home, we saw a young man coming up the road with a cast on his leg. Vickie said, "Why don't you ask him to come?" I walked up to the man and asked him if he went to church anywhere. He said that he had just gotten out of prison. I said, "Well, would you like to come to our church?" He said again, "I just got out of prison." I told him that I didn't care about that and asked if he had ever read the Bible. He explained to me that he had indeed been reading the Bible and had been doing so the entire two years he was in prison. I then asked him if he had ever asked God to come into his heart. When he revealed to me that he didn't know how to do that, I gave him a tract. I told him to find a quiet place by himself to read it and then say the prayer on the back page. I told him that I could offer him transportation to church, and he told me he could get there by himself, but thanked me anyway. The next day I looked for him and didn't see him. I waited until our worship service started and then made my way inside. I was thrilled to see him already inside the sanctuary. When the invitation came, he walked up to the altar and gave his life to Christ. Weeks later, when his cast was removed, he was baptized. I think back about that day I met him and how I was ready to give up, but God wasn't. Praise God.

*I have an old backhoe at Peace Valley and one day a cylinder started leaking. I took it off and took it to my friend Leon who has a repair shop. When I dropped it off, I told Leon that he didn't know me now because I was born again and I shared my testimony. Several days later, I went to pick up the cylinder and when I put it back on the backhoe, it was still leaking. I called Leon. He apologized and said to bring it back. When I arrived, he started working on it right away and when he finished, he used the air compressor to blow off the excess dirt. When he did this, an o-ring went flying. He got a new one, put it in and it fit perfectly. He then shared a story with me that proved once again that God is always in control. He said that the other day he had done the same thing, but he knew he didn't have a replacement o-ring that size so started searching frantically for the one that was lost. Just when he was about to give up, his wife walked out of the office sixty feet away and asked what he was doing. He told her what happened and she asked, "Did you look in that 5-gallon bucket of oil over there?" Leon said, "No." She said, "Well, that's where it is." Leon dumped the oil out of the bucket and sure enough, that's where he found the o-ring. My question is, did God have me drive over there three times, 180 miles to get that testimony, or did he have me go over there to share more of mine. If God cares about o-rings and nuts, I know that he cares about lost souls. Praise God!

*The state of Missouri wanted to purchase a strip of land on our property and had contacted me to meet with their representative up on the highway. When I arrived, I found a lady waiting for me and we discussed how much land was needed and how much they would pay me for it. Our conversation turned to belief in Jesus Christ and our faith. I asked if she wanted to hear my testimony and then told her of seeing the light of Heaven. She asked if I would meet with her again the next day and told me a time and location. When I arrived at home, I told my wife, Vickie, that I would not go back to meet with this lady unless she came with me. I told her that I felt she had a testimony she wanted to share. The next day, Vickie and I met with the woman and talked a while about the highway and then she said she believed that God brought me into her life. She then told me a story that she never told anyone before. She had a daughter who died at the age of thirteen and her anger with God was intense. She told us of how her daughter from the age of six would come and tell her that she heard God call her name and would talk to her. It had happened several times, but this woman never thought much about it until her daughter died. While coping with the loss of this child, she was lying in bed one night and heard music fill the room. It was the most beautiful music she had ever heard. She heard the same music for three more nights. She revealed to us that she took it as a sign from God that her daughter Shay was all right and with Him.

*My friend Paul attends a different church, but I received a message that he was in a hospital ninety miles away to have surgery for a hole in his heart. I called his room to check on him and was pleased to know that he was surrounded by his family and friends from church. He told me that tests had shown air bubbles going from one side of his heart to the other and he had also suffered a stroke. Paul had said to his nurse, "Maybe God will heal my heart." Two weeks later, I called Paul at his home to ask how he was. He informed me that he didn't have to have surgery because God had indeed healed the hole in his heart. He also said that the doctors couldn't find any reason for his stroke. I believe Paul went through what he did to glorify God.

*While working on a pig farm, a lady from our church was asked by the farm owner to help him give shots to a new sow he had just purchased. The whole time she was helping give the sow the medicine, the animal was sneezing and coughing. A week later, she started feeling sick with a headache and sore throat and thought it was allergies. On Christmas Eve, several weeks later, she was feeling horribly ill with high fever and vomiting and decided to go to bed early. The next morning her brother went into the bedroom to wake her up. As he shook her, she started crying and laughing in her sleep. Her brother and mother tried to pull her up by her arms and found them stiff and her eyes rolled back into her head. At this point, they called 911 and arranged to meet the ambulance halfway into town. At the hospital, she was put on life support and a spinal tap and other tests were performed. The doctors confirmed that she had meningitis and needed to transfer her to a hospital two hours away in St. Louis. During that transfer, she flat-lined twice and was brought back. Upon arriving in St. Louis, her family was told that she wouldn't live to see the morning and if she did, it would be on life support and in a vegetative state. She remained in a deep coma for a week. When she awoke, she found tubes and I.V. lines in her feet, arms, mouth and nose and then went into a deep sleep for several hours. When she awoke again, she saw her mom and several nurses. They smiled and told her that it was a miracle like they've never seen before; she should have been dead. The doctor came in a while later and informed her that the meningitis had eaten a hole in her eardrum, causing her brain to swell. She was released a few days later with the I.V. still in her arm and a weak heart valve caused by the infection. She gives praise to God for pulling her through.

*My friend Tommy was preaching on the back of a flatbed trailer to motorcycle riders, some of whom were members of Hell's Angels. As he started to preach, something came over him and he asked if someone in the audience was planning to commit a murder. A very tall man in the back came forward. Tommy, standing on the trailer, was looking this man straight in his eyes. Tommy asked if he was the one and the man said yes. Tommy then asked if he had a gun on him. The man pulled it out and laid it at Tommy's feet. Tommy asked the man if he still wanted to kill someone. When the man responded, "No", Tommy asked him if he wanted to change his ways and accept the Lord. The man said, "Yes." As Tommy bowed his head to start praying, no words would come out. Tommy stared at the man and then asked, "Do you have another gun?" The man pulled out the second pistol and laid it down as well. Tommy took a deep breath and was then able to pray. The man accepted Jesus and was changed right there. With excitement, the man called his wife to tell her the good news. She, however, was furious. She still wanted the person killed. The tall man returned and said, "I have to get back to North Carolina and settle this with my wife." In the meantime, God called on an 80-year-old lady and told her to go across the street and witness to the woman there. When she knocked on the door, it was opened by the biker's wife who asked what the elderly lady wanted. The woman replied, "God told me to come over." The old lady led the young wife to Christ. The next morning, when the tall man arrived at home, he and his wife rejoiced together and neither of them wanted anyone dead.

*On June 17, 1995 I woke up and was very sick. I got up and went into my living room and sat down on the fireplace hearth. As I was sitting there, I felt something break in my stomach. Vickie got up and asked what was wrong. I told her I thought I was going to die. She said, "I will call your doctor in St. Louis." I said, "All you will get is an answering machine." She tried and got no answer. I was in such pain I told her I was going to drown myself in the pond behind the house. She said, "I will call my doctor." I told her that no doctor is going to answer his phone at 6:30 a.m. on Father's Day morning. She called anyway and Dr. James answered his phone. He told us to meet him in the ER at the hospital and he would be there in 30 minutes. I started to put my pants on and I was so swelled they wouldn't even come close to going together. When we started down "V" Hwy, I was screaming in pain. When we got to I-44 she pulled off on the shoulder of the ramp. I asked her what we were stopping for. She said she didn't know what to do. I said, "Are we going to the hospital or not." She said yes. I said, "Well, put the petal to the metal." And she did. I looked over and we were going over 100 mph.

When we got to the ER, I was barely able to walk. I made it to the desk and asked the girl if she had a wheel chair. She looked shocked and said no. I asked her if she had anything to throw up in. She said no. I grabbed a trashcan and said that it would work. We took a seat. I think I said something like this: "God help me." The doctor showed up and took one look at me and said, "You need surgery right now." He turned and asked the desk lady if a surgeon and anesthesiologist were in the hospital. "There is one out in the parking lot ready to leave and one on the elevator going home." He said, "Go stop them. We have to get some blood out of him, but his veins are not showing." The nurse said, "There is a nurse upstairs that can get blood from anyone." He said to go get her. She came and was able to draw some blood. The anesthesiologist came and gave me a shot as I was walking toward surgery. When I woke up in ICU, the first thing I saw was my blue-eyed wife praying over me. I realize now that God had a plan for me. Praise God.

*My cousin was in a hospital about 150 miles from Rolla. She was being released the next day and her husband was going to pick her up. When he got there, he had to tell her that the car heater was not working. It had stopped about a week earlier. It was very cold and they didn't know how they were going to make it home without heat. She decided to pray, so she put her hands on the dash and called out to the Lord to fix the heater. He did and it hasn't stopped working since.

*Kenny Jones and I were gigging on a cold winter night in Jan. 2007. Gigging is a sport that you do at night with lights on the front of your boat and you spear fish with a long handled pronged spear. We were about a mile from the cabin. We started back up river and I put two 5-gallon buckets of water on the front deck of the boat for weight so the motor wouldn't hit the rocks. The temperature was 14 degrees. We got about a half mile from the cabin by a slough in the river. I reached out and gigged a small suckerfish. When I turned to put the fish in the boat, my heel hit one of the buckets. I fell out backwards and went all the way under water. When I came up, I was in water almost up to my neck. I started pulling the boat to shallow water. I was trying to get in the boat when Ken got me by the belt and helped me in. I landed in the fish box with the rest of the suckers. We started back to the cabin. I realized my hood and clothes were starting to freeze. We didn't hit one rock or anything all the way back to the cabin. I had a hot fire going in the wood stove. I could hardly talk without slurring my words. The rest of this story is: Ken Jones had cancer in 1986. He was not a Christian. Since then, he has found the Lord. My thought is that if he hadn't found the Lord and would have died of cancer and gone to Hell, I would have died in the river that night. Thank God for him. Thank God He cared for me. We were both in God's plan. Now we travel together and witness on the streets spreading the good news about God's love.

Hell

"And shall cast them into the furnace of fire;
there shall be wailing and gnashing of teeth."
Matthew 13:50

*My friend Ken told me about a dream he had where he saw people walking around in smoke that looked strange. There was a large lake. The people were young and old and most appeared dead or not moving. A young couple drove up in a car and asked him where they were. He told them they were in Hell. He saw a large man with huge chains around his legs and people lying in front of him. He called out to the Lord and a door opened into a hallway. He walked out and saw young people going in. Some were looking through a glass in the door, but could see nothing. I tried to stop them from going in, but I couldn't.

*I had the opportunity to speak at a testimony night on New Year's Eve at a church outside of Rolla. The pastor of the church waited until everyone else had shared his or her testimony and then he told us this. When he was about 14 years old, he felt the Lord calling him to preach and started to do so with the local kids he knew. One night, he had a dream or vision. He was standing on a hill and behind him was Hell. On a far-reaching hill in front of him, he saw a bright light with people moving towards him. As they got closer, he realized that he knew some of them and tried to turn them back towards the light. Some turned back and others just walked past him. He said that his back started to burn and he awoke startled. He got up and went to the kitchen and told his mother that his back was burning. She lit a lamp and lifted his nightshirt to discover his back was very red. His mother thought that he may have been standing too close to the wood stove until he told her of his vision. This man continued to preach and to help people be saved from the fires of Hell and has been doing so for more than 40 years.

*While in an office with a person, he asked if I would like to hear a testimony about Hell. I said sure because lots of people don't like to talk or even think about Hell. He said, "This man I know has a drinking problem. He said he woke up in Hell. He said he was chained to a cold stone wall with his face pushing against the wall so hard that he couldn't move. He said it was horrible."

*A very good Christian man told me he had a dream or vision. He said in this dream a beast was after him. The beast had two long curved teeth that were about 12 inches long. Every time he would stop, the beast would catch up and bite him in the head. He ran and ran, but couldn't get away. Finally he woke up. I think he was in Hell.

* Lola's testimony: I have been in church most of my life. In my 30's, I was straying from the Lord. I had a vision. The earth seemed like a huge carnival. I came upon a ladder and I started climbing. About half way up I heard a voice that said, "Lola, come down." I looked around and saw no one and took a couple more steps up. I heard the voice again and again saying the same thing. I looked and saw no one near. I took one more step and could see over the top that it was a slide. I saw people shoving themselves down the slide, with people right behind, their feet right up against the other person's back. They were screaming. Before I started

up the ladder, I thought they were yelling because they were having fun. But when I saw them going down the slide I realized they were screaming in terror and pain from the heat they were feeling as they were sliding down into a blue blazing lake of fire. The voice said, "Lola, do you want to go there?" I realized it was the Lord speaking, I said, "No, Lord" and came back down the ladder. I got back in church and began serving the Lord. I am now an ordained minister of the gospel of Jesus Christ.

PRAYER

"And all things, whatsoever ye shall ask in prayer, believing, ye shall receive." Matthew 21:22

* A preacher named Danny told me a testimony about prayer. He was doing construction work when he got a call asking him to come to the hospital to pray for a lady about to have surgery. He drove his work crew over to the large hospital and was informed by the doctor that the woman would be having a large gallstone removed. Danny and his crew immediately started praying that God would heal the woman. After discussion, they decided to go home to clean up and would return to be with the woman before she went into surgery. While still at home, Danny received a call from the hospital. The woman's doctor had done another x-ray and couldn't find any stones or anything wrong. She was released and went home the same day. Praise God.

*While passing out water for the Baptist Association at the State Fair, a man approached our tent and asked us to pray for him. His name was Lanny. He told us that his wife of 22 years wanted a divorce and that he and his 17-year-old son didn't want it to happen. He asked that we pray that his marriage be restored to the way God had brought it together. Another man working in the tent stopped witnessing to the young people and joined me to pray for this man. All three of us got down on our knees in the misty rain and prayed. After our prayer, we met Lanny's son and assured him that our church would pray for them. About a month later, a preacher named Larry was in town to do a revival at our church. He had agreed to go with me to witness door to door. When I went to pick him up at his hotel, he was on the phone. After he finished his call, he told me that he had good news. He told me of a man from his hometown that had gone to every church he could and asked for prayer that his marriage be restored. His situation had advanced to the point that he had to hire an attorney to make sure he and his son's interest would be protected. The divorce papers were ready to be signed, but when the wife picked up the pen to finalize them, she started crying and said she couldn't do it. I said to Larry, "Is the man's name Lanny, and does he have a 17-year-old son?" Larry said, "How could you possibly know that?" I told him about praying for him a month earlier at the fair. Larry exclaimed, "You're the one!" He said that Lanny had told him of our meeting and that two men had prayed with him, on their knees, in the rain. Larry asked me if I would give that testimony to begin our revival. I told him I wouldn't be able to keep my mouth shut about it. Larry then hit redial on his phone and I found myself talking to the man I had prayed with a month ago. A month after the revival, I talked to Larry and he informed me that Lanny, his wife and son came to his church and accepted the Lord and joined the church. Praise God!

*My friend Ken and I were in Paoni, Colorado and had stopped in a store to buy supplies. We must have looked lost because another shopper asked if we needed help. We told her we were looking for pancake mix for dummies. We also asked her if she went to church. She said she did and was Catholic. For some strange reason, I asked if she had anything wrong with her. She did; it was a brain tumor. She seemed stunned that two old men would care about her. Ken and I asked if she wanted us to pray for her and she did. Right there in the store, we prayed that she would be healed by God and that her doctors would be guided by Him. She was very happy that we cared. I still don't know why we asked if anything was wrong with her, but I do know that God works in many ways.

*Ken and I were back into that same store later where we approached a woman and asked if she went to church. She told us that she stopped going because they made her feel as if she didn't belong. She revealed that her mother goes to a church ten miles away. We had prayer for her and told her to drive over and go to church with her mom. Praise God, He set me free and now I can talk openly to people about Him.

*My mother died in her home on July 9, 2005. Vickie, Judy, Roger, Joy and Cierra were singing *"One Day At A Time"* as she went to be with the Lord in Heaven. After her death, we cleaned the house carpet and closed it up. About a month went by and Vickie and I started to discuss what we should do with the house, which was on our property between our house and Vickie's mother's house. Another two weeks went by before we decided to rent the house out. We drove in the driveway one day and we stopped and went into the house. I told Vickie that if we are going to rent this house, I wanted to get God involved as to whom we should rent it to. We got down on our knees at Mom's bed and prayed our list to God. We asked for a Christian couple or single lady who doesn't smoke or drink and could be a friend to Mildred, Vickie's mother. A week later, Vickie was speaking with a lady in a neighboring town and told her of our prayers for Mom's house. She said, "I think I know the perfect lady." A couple of days later, Glenda, a non-smoking, Christian showed up. She and Mildred get along great. Glenda now helps Mildred when we are away from home and they feed the fish in the pond together. She has also joined our church, is wonderful with the children and teaches the pre-school.

Vickie and I have been blessed by God. What a wonderful God we serve.

*As we entered the church for Christmas Eve service, a bird flew in the door. Nine of us tried for twenty minutes to get the bird back outside. We finally gave up and started our service. It was decided that I would come back in the morning when it was light, and try again to help the bird find its way out. Christmas morning, I returned with a leaf blower and a net thinking that it might help move the bird towards a door or window. The bird flew over and over again from the exit sign above the door to the cross behind the altar. I finally fell down in prayer, asking God to guide the bird outside because I didn't want to hurt it. Just then, the bird flew to a window. It just watched me as I walked towards it and whistled. Then it flew toward a window by the organ. I whistled at the bird again and it flew towards me and then turned and flew out the door. I fell to my knees with tears of joy streaming down my face for the love and power of God. He has complete control of everything and had done what nine of us couldn't do the night before. When I was on my way to the church that morning, I thought I was going to let the bird out and maybe someone would be waiting who was cold, hungry or just needing to hear the gospel. I didn't realize I was going to receive a gift from God. Thank you, Lord, King of Kings and Lord of Lords. When I laid down the net and got on my knees, that's when God went to work. God showed me He could do it if I just humbled myself by falling down and calling out to the One and only God of the Universe. A bird came to church to the light. A bird came to church to lift us up. A bird came to church to show us Jesus cares.

*God works not only in mysterious ways, but appears in mysterious places. In a busy office, could God penetrate the confusion of telephones, computers and noisy bustle to perform His miracles? Yes. Consider the story of the man in the office. In his own words he said, "I was not happy in my work and thought about quitting, but I have children in college and need a job to pay for their education. I became desperate and needed help. I would go out to my barn at home and get down on my knees and call out to the Lord to help me. I've never been very close to my daughter who is away at college. Last July, I went to the Lord and prayed that she and I would grow closer together. Two days later, my wife and I got a call from her asking if she could come home for the weekend. When she arrived home, she put her arms around me and hugged me. We've been getting along fine ever since that day. My prayers were answered. I am now going to a good church. I enjoy going to work and my business has picked up. I believe that God wants me to be in this busy office to bear witness to His love."

*I struck up a conversation with a woman at a yard sale. I shared my testimony with her and then she shared hers. She said that her son worked at the Pentagon and arrived at work one day to find that his I.D. card would not work. He said it made him real mad. He reported it and was told someone would check out the problem. The next day he tried again to use the card, but it still wouldn't work and he again went home very mad. That day was September 11, 2001. Twenty-three of his co-workers and friends were killed on that day. He called his mother and said, "Your prayers have been answered." He is now back in church every Sunday.

*Larry was back in town for another revival at our church. Saturday morning, we went to the local hospital to call on some people. When we arrived, we found a lady with a flat tire in the parking lot. Larry told her we would take it to be fixed since she didn't have a spare. When we returned, we struck up a conversation while putting her tire back on. We asked where she was from and if she went to church. Her home was 30 miles away and she did attend church. Her boyfriend was in the hospital and she had slept in her car, not knowing that there was a place in the hospital for family to sleep. For some reason, we asked if she was troubled by something. She said, "I think I have a demon inside me." We asked if she wanted prayer and she said yes. Larry used the anointing oil I had with me and poured some on her head. I got down on my knees and called out to God to bind Satan from her. Larry did the same with his hands on her head. When she left us, she was jumping two feet high all the way to the hospital door. Praise God!

*Our church was having a revival and the evangelist, Larry, was due to arrive in town at 3:00 pm. Around 2:00, I told Vickie that I wanted to go up to a trailer park not far from our home and invite people to come. I went to the first five trailers, but no one was home. At the sixth, the door was opened by a lady who was about thirty-five years old. I asked if she went to church anywhere and she said, "No, not now." I asked her if she had ever asked Jesus into her life and she said, "yes." Then I asked if she had been baptized and she said, "no." When I gave her one of my cards, she told me that she had brought her two children to our church several years before. "Wait here just a minute," she told me. When she returned, she had one of my cards in her hand and asked if Vickie was my wife. She remembered us because Vickie had been so kind to her kids and she was always curious about my card that read "God Spoke To Me." I asked if something was wrong and as she started to cry, she told me that someone was mistreating her son. We started to pray together and she became calm again. About that time, Larry called to say he had arrived at the church. I asked the woman if it was alright to bring Larry back with me in a few minutes and I would share my testimony. When we got back, I introduced them and then we sat on her deck and I told her what God had done and said to me. Larry prayed for her and we left. She came to our Sunday service for the next two weeks and then came forward and asked to be baptized. She and her children continued to participate with our church and, a year later, I baptized both children. Praise God for the Holy Spirit.

   *A woman at our church gives this testimony. "I was starting my life over at the age of 41. I could give you the background, but that would be a book in itself, so I'll just start with meeting Bryan. When we met, I was working three jobs including bartending. I was hired by the company that had brought him to Texas to work. At Bryan's prompting, the site manager trained me in many areas of their work that I originally was not hired to perform. Within a month, I was working full-time with the company and was able to quit my job bartending. Although I was set on remaining single and independent, Bryan and I began to spend time together away from work and developed a very strong friendship. He told my then 20-year-old daughter, that even if we were never more than friends, his goal was to get me away from bartending permanently. I knew I cared deeply for Bryan, but I was a divorced woman with a mixed up life and a lot of regrets of bad decisions. While keeping him at arms length, I was praying diligently for guidance. I asked God to put an obstacle between Bryan and me if the relationship was not in His plan for us. We moved to Colorado with the company and during the next eight to nine months we met members of each other's family and friends and were finding common ground in our relationship with the Lord. I found the more I grew spiritually, the closer Bryan and I became. After many lengthy conversations we discovered that we had both been praying for the same thing, that God make His will for us known. We realized that we had already both committed our hearts to each other and decided to marry. We asked Kenny Campbell to perform the ceremony. Before joining Bryan's church, I received spiritual counseling, professed my faith in Jesus Christ as my Savior, and was baptized. My Catholic upbringing never came close to the love and acceptance I felt at Second Baptist Church. Bryan and I were married there on

September 21st. I am a different woman than I was when I met him—I'm better. The idea I had of a good marriage and good husband are completely dwarfed by what I have now. God has blessed me in ways I never knew existed. The more I work on my personal relationship with the Lord, the better all my relationships become. I often start crying because my heart is overflowing with so much joy. I know that God brought Bryan into my life and Bryan helped me to know God more fully. I couldn't have found either one without the other. I stopped praying for what I wanted and started praying for God's will to be done. He knows me and my needs better than I do."

PROTECTION

*"For he shall give his angels charge over thee,
to keep thee in all thy ways."*
Psalms 91:11

✱ In 1972, Vickie and I were traveling around Australia. We had camped at Berry Springs in the "outback" in the northern part. Around 10:00 pm, a young man, who had pitched a tent in the same park, knocked on our camper door. He and his friend were having trouble sleeping because a snake was moving around under their ground sheet and wanted help to get it out. They told me that the snake would make its way under the tent every night when the air temperature started getting cold. I picked up a large stick on my way over to the tent and when the two fellows pulled it back, I hit and killed the snake. The next morning I measured the snake; it was eight feet long and its head was two inches across. I thought to myself, no wonder these guys couldn't sleep. I don't know if the snake was poisonous or not, but most found in Australia are. If it had bitten me, I probably would've died from sheer fright.

*While still in Australia, we made our way from Melbourne to Perth. A National Geographic map I had showed some caves relatively close to where we were on Nullabar Plain. We drove out and found one that was supposed to have an underground lake below completely flat country. I got a makeshift ladder and started down into the cave with just a small flashlight. It got very dark very fast. I started picking up and throwing rocks ahead of me so I would not walk off into the lake. I had gone about 200 yards when I heard a splash from the rock I threw. I walked up to the edge of the lake and shined my flashlight downward. Because the water was so clear, I couldn't tell where the water began. I turned back, found the ladder and climbed out. I believe by that time Vickie was getting a little worried. I never gave any thought to the possibility that my flashlight could've gone out. Nor did I think about getting hurt until we got back to the car and I realized that had there been an accident, the car keys were in my pocket. Vickie would have been stranded, several miles off the highway in extreme heat. Praise God-He was looking out for me.

*I was traveling on the Yukon River, going from the Bering Sea to Fairbanks, Alaska. I stopped in Marshall, Alaska to find fuel. I walked the quarter mile up a steep hill to the store and filled my six-gallon can. On my way back, I took a different route and ended up finding a path at the bottom of yet another steep hill. Feeling adventurous, I made my way down to this new path and started heading back to the river. I didn't notice the wooden boxes on either side of the path until a dog came running full speed towards me, barking loudly. Just short of reaching me, the dog hit the end of his chain. I realized that all the boxes had dogs in them and I found myself walking between them with another 150 feet to go. I thought about opening the gas can and pouring it out in front of me, but I didn't. I just made sure that I walked a straight line out of there. This whole time the dogs were barking, snapping and stretching out as far as the chains would let them. If just one chain or collar had broken, I would have been killed. God had a plan for me and it wasn't to be eaten by dogs.

*When I camped in Alaska, I usually left my food in the boat. This time I got my tent out and sleeping bag open. The next thing I heard was a bear outside my tent. As he growled and barked at me, I jumped straight up, not knowing whether he would come through the side or not. I picked up my 22-caliber rifle and stuck it out through a hole in the zipper. When I pulled the trigger, it snapped. I jacked another shell in the barrel and it fired this time. I listened and didn't hear anything more. I read my Bible and then lay down and went to sleep. God had His hand on me. As I was going back up the river toward Russian Mission, a strong wind came up on me. It was a miracle I didn't drown in the river. The water was really cold and there was still snow on some of the gravel bars. I got up river about 40 miles and I decided to cross to the other side. I came out from behind an island and the winds were so strong I was afraid if I tried to turn back, I would turn the boat over. The river was about three to five miles wide and I was in waves about 3 ft high. My boat was a 36-inch bottom Jon boat and 14 feet long. I was carrying seven tanks of fuel and all my gear. I was in trouble. I looked across the river and saw a boat. As I got closer, I realized it was a fishing boat that was two stories high and the spray was going over it. I kept my boat floating with the engine. I was hoping that I could land on the other bank and then, as I got closer, I realized it was a high bank with no place to land. Finally, I saw a break in the cliff and I headed for it. As I got close to the bank, the wind got even stronger. It actually was blowing me backwards with my engine running forward. It blew me backward into the bank. I raised the engine and ran into the ground at the same time. Thank God He cared for me. I went on to Russian Mission, sold my boat and flew out. I had been 38 days on the river.

*In 1976, I bought a new truck and installed a cab-over camper on it. Vickie and I were on our first trip to Alaska and headed towards Glacier Park, Montana. As we hit the flatlands, the winds were getting stronger and stronger the closer we got to the mountains. Because we were heading straight into the wind, it felt like the camper was being pulled off the truck. I told Vickie that we would have to stop and do something about it. I found a place to pull over and got out of the truck. It was so windy that I could hardly make it around the rear of the truck. I looked around and saw some big rocks. After clearing the camper floor, I loaded several 100-pound rocks and then continued on our journey. We finally made it to the campground in a National Park and the ranger at the gate looked shocked. He asked what we were driving and I stated a truck with a cab-over camper. He said he didn't know how on earth we made it because the winds were topping 92 mph and had turned over several semi-trailers during the afternoon. My wife admits to me now that she was very scared and had been praying for our safety during that drive. Thank God I married her!

*As I started writing this book, Vickie reminded me of an experience we had in Canada. We were about 600 miles north of Winnipeg fishing on Lake Notigi. It was about 6:00 p.m. when the wind started blowing harder and we thought we'd better head to our campground. The only problem was that the 5½ HP motor on the boat wouldn't start. We decided to find shelter on the shore, but didn't have anything to get under. We built a fire, and then tried to build a lean-to with sticks and leafy branches. As I worked on the engine, it was becoming darker outside, but fortunately the wind started to subside. I managed to get the motor started on one cylinder, and that was enough to attempt our return to camp several miles a way. By the time we got back into the boat, there was neither moon nor stars to be seen. Off in the distance, I saw a tower with a blinking light. I knew if I kept that tower to my left, I would be heading to the truck. By the time we arrived at our camp, it was after 11:00 pm. We were wet, but alive. After 25 years, when I talked to Vickie about our adventure that day, I asked her if she had been afraid. She said yes, but she just prayed to God for our safety. Vickie has stood by me whenever we were in trouble. I know that God put her in my life and if it hadn't been for her and her walk with Him, I probably would have died and gone to Hell.

*Back in the 60's, I was building a small home in Meadow Brook. I was working by myself on framing a wall in the middle of the house. It was over 30 ft long. I was young and strong and stupid. I got it all ready to raise and put it up on blocks. I grabbed it like a weight lifter and when I picked it up and flipped it, I grabbed two studs on each side of me and both of them snapped. It came down with such force that the broken studs stabbed through the plywood flooring on each side of me. If either one had stabbed me, I would have died. God protected me again.

*When Vickie and I bought our river property, we named it Peace Valley. We asked our pastor to come down and bless it for the glory of God. At that time, we also asked God to protect the property and anyone who came on it. We dedicated it to God because we realize that we own nothing. Everything we have is given to us by God; we are just stewards. We anointed every entrance to the property including those by road, path and river. We also anointed the house with oil and prayer. After conferring with Vickie about how it was done in the Bible, I started collecting stones to build an altar. I prayed about it, and then built my altar in a half moon shape with the largest of thirteen stones in the middle and the other twelve around it. I then placed a cross at the center stone, facing east. We decided to anoint our personal property back in town as well. We asked God to keep us from harm and to keep hate from being brought in. As with the river house, we anointed all entrances into the house and roads coming on the property. Six months later, we invited a man to come over for breakfast on a Saturday morning. He showed up at about 8:00 am, looking strange and a bit shaken. I thought he might be sick or something. When we finished eating, he said he needed to talk with me. We walked to the shed and as we entered, he went over and kicked the tire of my tractor. He kicked so hard, it shook the 10,000 lb. rig. When prompted for an explanation, he said he was mad about something someone did to his daughter. He told me, as he entered our property that morning, something came over him. He thought he was having a heart attack. He had to stop his car for a while until he was able to drive. I asked if he had hate in him, and then explained that when we anointed it, we asked God not to allow hate on our property. The man said he didn't know what it was, but assured me that it worked.

*In 1987, I was driving to the Yukon Territory in Canada, pulling my Jon boat. When my truck lost power, I pulled off the road. The engine was still running, but not pulling. I looked in the rear view mirror and saw the back axle and wheel were out about 18 inches. A nut had come loose and a tube on the axle was bent. I didn't know what to do. I was eighty miles from town on the Alaskan highway. Then God gave me a thought. I got a coil of soft wire and wrapped it in the threads where the nut had been. I started beating on the wire and after about two and a half long hours later, I was able to put another nut on. I thank God that I had an earthly father who showed me a lot of important things in life. It has been more than 22 years and I'm still using that same truck at Peace Valley.

*Vickie and I were fishing on Notigi Lake and saw a small outlet. We saw a trail that went to a small lake and decided to go and fish in it. The old trail was grown up with bushes and brush. It was probably a trail used by the Indians to trap and hunt. We were moving along the trail when we heard a loud growl. There was a large bear on its hind legs about 70 ft. from us. Vickie said. "Should we run?" I replied, "No, we're going to stand and fight." As I pulled my filet knife out, the bear started running at us full speed. It stopped suddenly about 30 ft. away from us, growled and made a horrific scream. I then screamed back at it as loud as I could and Vickie said she heard another bear making noise. The bear we could see got down on all fours again and walked away. Maybe the bear thought we were between her and her cub. It wasn't in God plan for us to be eaten by a bear.

*While elk hunting in Colorado on Spruce Mountain, I prepared a place to sleep for the night. I dug a hole in the soft ground by a spruce tree, lay down and covered up with some plastic sheeting. Around 2:00 am, I heard a limb break. I woke up to find elk running and jumping all around me. I don't know how they missed stepping on me, but if they had, I would've certainly been killed. God protected me again; He had a plan for me.

*Ken and I were coming back from a trip on the Yukon River and were driving through Wyoming, pulling a boat behind the truck. We decided to stop for the night and I told Ken I would guide him into a parking spot. I got out and stood on the passenger side of the truck to direct him. I heard a hissing noise and told him we must have a tire going flat. Ken said, "That's no flat; that's a rattlesnake." Everyone knows when you guide a driver and vehicle; you stand on the driver's side. If I had moved to the correct side to do so, I would've been bitten. Since we were 60 miles from the nearest town, I probably would've died. Again, God's protective hand was over me.

*On one of our trips to Australia, Vickie and I stopped to camp for the night near the bank of a muddy river. Vickie started making sandwiches for dinner and I told her I would go and try to catch some fish. I set up on the bank and when she called me to come eat, I tied my pole to a bush. When I went back after eating to check on the pole, I was shocked. The tide had gone out and there was a big print left by a crocodile just four feet from where I had been sitting. Vickie said I was very pale when I came back to the camper. God was protecting me again.

*My 89-year-old mother and I were at the river cabin one afternoon. I had just come off the river when I looked to the sky and saw a storm coming. I used my truck to pull the boat out of the water and had just gotten back to the cabin when the storm hit. All of a sudden, a tornado came down the center of the river and Mom and I watch it go by. We saw trees breaking and falling on both sides of the river and the air was full of debris. A tree about 10 ft. from my deck bent completely over the electric lines and touched the handrail near us, but didn't break. Mom and I just stood there and never moved. We never even felt any wind hit us. After it was over, I went around looking at the damage. A barn was torn down on the other side of the river and metal was scattered for a quarter mile. As I walked down to the boat ramp, I had to crawl over trees and branches to get to the water. I went back up to my cabin to check for any damage there. In front of the cabin, I saw my truck, boat and backhoe. There was not a single scratch or dent on any of them and no damage to the cabin either. It seemed as if the tornado split and went around our cabin. I know God's hand protected us. For about a mile and a half I had to push about 60 trees out of the road to get to the highway.

RIGHT PLACE-RIGHT TIME

"And as they led him away, they laid hold upon one Simon, a Cyrenian, coming out of the country, and on him they laid the cross, that he might bear it after Jesus."
Luke 23:26

✱Vickie and I have been to Australia five times over the past 35 years. In the '80's, we flew to Melbourne and then drove to Perth in a rental car. It was a long trip across 2000 miles of hot desert in a car with no air-conditioning. We were traveling about 80 mph that early morning when we saw people standing on the highway. We stopped to find out what was happening and found a young couple with a small baby looking towards their car at the bottom of a steep bank. The woman had swerved to avoid a kangaroo and the car ran off the road. It was on its roof and the tires were still turning. The car was new and the couple had all their belongings in it. In Australia, if you leave your car by the roadside, it's fair game for anyone who comes upon it. We knew we had to help these people. I spoke with several others who had stopped as well and told them that I thought we could turn the car upright and drive it up the bank. When they questioned whether it was possible, I said, "I know we can." One man said to the others, "This Yank says we can turn the car over and drive it out." And with that, we all took hold of the car and rolled it up on its side and then pushed it again up on its wheels. It hit so hard it blew out two tires. Within a few minutes the blown tires were coming off and spares were being put on. The man who owned the car asked if I would start the engine and make sure it would be okay. I turned the key in the ignition and it started up like nothing had ever happened. He then asked if I would drive the car up the steep bank as he was fearful he would not be able to do so himself. The car went up the hill without a problem. The couple started to rearrange their belongings and when they opened the trunk of the car, we saw that they were carrying two, six-gallon cans of gas. Of course, everyone always carries extra gas traveling across the big desert, but if those cans had caught fire during the accident, it would have been disastrous. I think God had His hand on me and put me in the right place and the right time to say, "We can." Thank God, no one was hurt.

*My ministry is going to hospitals or nursing homes and visiting people from our church, or their loved ones. One morning my friend Dale and I were heading to a St. Louis hospital to pray for a church member, Judy, who was having surgery that morning at 5:30 am. We left very early and started on our way, wanting to be there for her before she was moved from her room. During our drive, I told Dale that we may not be going on this visit just for our church member. God may have someone else in mind. When we arrived and asked for directions to Judy's room, a woman told us she would show us the way. We prayed with Judy and then made our way to the waiting room. Before the lady left us, I asked if she went to church. She said she did, but could seldom get her husband to go with her. When he did attend, he couldn't wait to get out and get back home. They've been married for thirty-five years and she was about ready to give up on him. I explained to the lady, whose name was Judy as well, that my wife had prayed for me for forty-five years and that she shouldn't give up. I told her that although Dale and I had come to visit our church member Judy, we felt that God may bring us to someone else who may need to hear our good news. We talked with her some more and she told us about her family. Her husband was disabled and wouldn't touch a Holy Bible. Her daughter was too busy to go to church and her adopted son had just gotten into a fist-fight the night before with her husband. We offered to pray for her and her family and did so right then and there. When we were done, Judy had tears running down her cheeks and I knew Dale was touched. God put us where we needed to be at just the right time. As I go though life, I know God is in control of everything. I got my business card, and asked her to write the names of her family members so we could have our church pray for them. Since I am not good with names at all, I found it interesting that this lady's name was the same as the lady we were visiting from church. Judy's daughter's name is also the same shared by Dale's daughter. I think God planned this so we wouldn't forget their names.

The following week, I returned to the hospital with Pastor Leroy to check on our church member. I decided to take copies of testimonies I had collected and to give them to Judy for her husband. Although she wasn't working that day, I was assured that she would get them. I attached my business card and a tract to the package and went on my way. A few days later, I received a call from Judy saying that she had received the package and had given the tract to a man at work. She told me that this co-worker was 72 years old and several people had tried to talk to him about God, but he was never interested. After she gave him the tract, he came to work the next day a completely different man. People at work couldn't believe the change in him. While it was my intention to help a church member, it was God's will that I help two complete strangers. Later that day, I went to our local hospital to visit another church member. While waiting to see her, a man came up and started talking about his wife and her struggle with cancer. He told me that God had spared his life years prior when he fell fifteen feet and broke his back. He told me he was a member of the First Baptist Church in a neighboring town and I offered to have our church pray for him. We then prayed for his wife right then and there. He seemed to be very happy that I would do that. A few minutes later, I went in to see our church member. I told her that I thought I was coming to see her, but that God had a man that I was supposed to try and lift up with prayer. Several weeks passed and Vickie and I had received calls from Judy up in the St. Louis hospital asking for prayer for her, her family and one particular cancer patient. She told us that neither this patient nor his family was saved and she wanted to help them. One day, Judy called to ask for prayer for her adopted son and told us of the death of her cancer patient. She said because of our prayers, she got the courage to speak with the man about Jesus and he accepted the Lord prior to his death. She said she knew it was God who had put Dale and me into her life that day. This is another life saved by God putting us where we needed to be.

*Ken Jones and I were going from Molina, Co. to Cedar Ridge, Co. We stopped in a visitor center on the Grand Mesa to find out about the churches in Cedar Ridge that was about 20 miles away. I asked a young woman about the hours of the church services. She knew there were two or three churches there, but didn't know when they met. She didn't go to church. I gave her a short testimony. Then I told her boss that I guess I shouldn't be bothering her about church while she was working. He said that no, that's fine. I told him I was 66 years old when I was truly born again. He said, "Would you like to hear my testimony? I was an atheist at age 23. Then I became an agnostic. Then I picked up a Bible and started reading the book of Matthew. I read from the back to the front. When I got to the front of Matthew I knew that Jesus was who He said He

was. I am now a pastor and preach in a church in Austin, Co."
He also said I was in the 10% bracket of people to have been
born again at the age of 66. I think that he was happy that I
talked to his co-worker. The law now probably would not let
him mention anything about God while at work.

* We were traveling up the west coast of Australia in
1972 in a VW Combie Van. We were going to travel around
Australia. We would stop and fish off the piers and jetties
of various towns along the coast. We were at the town of
Dampier and decided to fish there. We were on the pier and
just started fishing when we saw a large fish come after our
bait, but he wouldn't take it. There were two guys that came
on the pier. We told them about the large fish and just about
that time, one of the guys spotted it. They ran back and got
their fishing equipment. They blew up a balloon and attached
it to their line. They baited it with a squid. When they threw
it out, the large fish hit it. They fought it for a while and then
pulled it over by the pier. We were about 10 or 12 ft. above
the water. One of the guys said, "I will climb down and get
the fish by the gills." He climbed down over the edge and was
climbing down the angle brace on the pier. As he reached out
to get hold of the fish, he slipped and fell in the ocean. When
he came back up, he grabbed hold of the pier post and then a
large wave picked him up while he had his arms around the
pole. It raised him up about 3 ft., and then dropped him when
the wave went down. All the sharp barnacles had cut him up
and down on his arms and chest. The other guy said, "We
have to get him out because of the blood that will bring the
sharks. There are a lot of sharks in these waters." So I helped
the man and we got over the side of the pier and managed to
get hold of him and help him out of the water. After we got
him out, they headed for a hospital or nurses station. I didn't
see them again, but God put me there at the right time. Later
that evening, Vickie caught a small shark and a sea snake.
Needless to say, we quit fishing for the night.

GOD'S SENSE OF HUMOR

*"And the Lord opened the mouth of the ass, and
she said unto Balaam, What have I done unto
thee, that thou hast smitten me these three times?"*
Numbers 22:28

✱Our pastor, Leroy, was in I.C.U. in Springfield,
Missouri for forty-two days. I would take someone
with me twice a week to visit him. I realized it wasn't only
Leroy that God was taking me there to see. Often I would
pray for and with people in the waiting rooms. I met a woman
whose husband had seven operations on his stomach. I asked
her if she went to church and she said, "Not regularly." I
told her to get back in church and meet some people and she
would find new friends who would be happy to sit and pray
with her at the hospital. When asked if I would visit and
pray with her husband, Virgil, I told her I would during my
next visit. When I returned the next time, I brought my wife,
Vickie. We started our visit with Leroy and found a nurse in
his room attending to him. We asked if she went to church
and she told us she used to. She was Presbyterian and her
husband Catholic. He was stronger in his faith and church,
so she went along with him once in a while. I mentioned the
Bible to her and she said it was like the game of "gossip".
Children start a story and tell it around in a circle in whispers

and then the last child tells what he heard out loud, which, of course, is always different from how it started. Vickie and I just looked at each other. I had trouble keeping my mouth shut. We were unable to check on Virgil that day, but would try again during our next visit. When we arrived the next time, we were told that he was taking a bath. I told the ladies on the nursing staff that I would wait and then handed them my business card that says, "GOD SPOKE TO ME", so they would have my name. While in the waiting room, a woman came looking for me, carrying my card. Guess what? It was the atheist nurse from the last visit. She wasn't looking too friendly when she asked if I knew Virgil. When I told her that I had never met him, she asked me why I wanted to see him. I explained that we knew his wife and she requested that we pray for him. The nurse finally relented and then warned us to ask him first if he wanted prayer. I introduced myself to Virgil and told him his wife wanted us to pray for him. I offered to leave if he wanted me to, but he said, "I want prayer." When I left his room, I noticed my business card on a table outside his door. I started laughing and praising the Lord. "God has a sense of humor," I said over and over. I went to see Virgil several more times and found that he was to be moved to a hospital near his home for another six weeks. The next time I stopped in to see him, he said, "I'm sure glad to see you. I'm going home." I said, "To the other hospital?" He said, "No, to my home." His seven previous operations and prayer had taken care of his problems. That's the power of God.

*After God called my name and freed me from hate, I was fired up. I would stop at any church, if I saw a car in the parking lot, and would go in and give my testimony to anyone who would listen. I stopped one day at a church about 25 miles from my home and went in and introduced myself to the pastor and another man. I offered to share my testimony and they said they would like to hear it. I spoke for about 20 minutes and then at the end of my story, I shouted out, "I'm free! I'm free! I'm free!" I heard people running up the stairs behind me. When I turned, I saw a teacher and about 15 kids staring at me in disbelief. The pastor laughed and told them everything was fine and to go back to class. He then offered to walk me out and asked the man he was with to wait for him. When we got out by my car, he thanked me for coming in and sharing my testimony. He felt strongly that the man inside needed to hear how Jesus set me free. Sometimes you don't know whom you are going to touch.

GOD'S PLAN

*"For I know the thoughts that I think toward you,
saith the Lord, thoughts of peace, and not of evil,
to give you an expected end."*
Jeremiah 29:11

✳ After hearing about Hurricane Katrina, I told Vickie that I wanted to go to Gulfport, Mississippi to help the victims. I'd spoken to a man named Rick who said his church had sent a group down there to help out and I decided to go also. I loaded up my trunk with tools and took off. When I made my first stop at a rest area, I inquired about motels and was told to stop in Hattiesburg, 85 miles north of Gulfport, as everything further south was rented out. When I arrived in Hattiesburg, I found the cheapest room available was $80.00 a night. The next day, I drove on to Gulfport and looked for the church group Rick had told me about, but couldn't find them. Next, I drove to the coast and was shocked to see the devastation cause by the power of Katrina. I had been told that a wave 30 to 40 feet high had hit the First Baptist Church, tearing off the front of the building and the vents out of the steeple, leaving only the back of the building intact. I drove east on towards Biloxi where I had been stationed many years ago. I pulled into a parking lot only to discover that it was a casino already up and running.

After praying that God take it down again, I drove by a house that was being rebuilt. I noticed a van sitting there with the North Carolina Baptist Association (NCBA) logo. I stopped and talked to three men who were working. They asked what I was doing there and I said it seemed like God told me to come. They informed me that I was welcome to stay at the Armory with them if I couldn't find other accommodations. I drove back to Gulfport, wishing that I had gotten better directions from Rick as to where the crews from his church were working. I ended up finding a motel with a vacant room and was charged $105.00 for a single. They were over-charging all those people who had lost their homes as well as others in town who came to help out. The next day, I checked out of the hotel and went in search of the Armory. When I found it, I went in and met Martha. She asked what I could do and I told her. I offered her my Driver's License so she could do a background check and 30 minutes later I was offered an air-conditioned room and supplied with bed linens and towels. I went to work on a new kitchen along side of a man who was Jewish. It was a real joy to work with him because he was very knowledgeable about the Bible. The first Sunday night, I got the opportunity to speak at a fairly large church and give my testimony. I was very impressed with all the people I was working with. Martha and her husband had signed up to work for two years as volunteers. They were among about 300 people who donated their time from the NCBA. With them they brought their own trailers, trucks, vans, storage units, forklifts and tools. I worked with them for ten days before returning home. About four months later, a man named Tony came to visit our church. While reading the visitor's card he filled out, Vickie noticed that he was from North Carolina. I asked him what brought him to our church. He said he just felt good when he pulled in the parking lot. He told us that he and his wife had separated and she moved back into the town with their two children. Since he didn't want to be away from

his children, he moved here, too. I asked if he had heard of
NCBA and he said he was a member. I told him of my time
with them in Gulfport and of Martha taking care of me. He,
too, had worked with them out of the same Armory just two
months after I did. Tony is now a member of our church. He
is a teacher, van driver and youth group leader. He is also a
member of Gideon International. There are no accidents or
luck involved when it comes to God's plan. The Lord put
Tony in our church. Praise God.

*I've known Larry, the evangelist, for about three years.
He has preached at our church revivals many times. I told
him that my friend Ken and I would come to his town in
Lewisburg, Kentucky and go out on the streets to invite
people to his church. The first thing we did when we arrived
was to go to the City Hall and get a street map. This way, we
could track where we went. While at City Hall, we talked to
several people and asked if they went to church. Some said
they did, others didn't even answer us. As we left, a man
about 40 years old followed us out. He said he was saved
in 2001 after terrorists blew up the World Trade Center on
9/11. I asked if he had followed in baptism and he said no.
He started telling us about his girlfriend and how she was
arrested for DWI and had just gotten out of jail. While in jail,
he said she met a Christian woman and talked about her kids
a lot. I told him if he was sleeping with his girlfriend out of
marriage, he was sinning. He said he knew that and it was
eating him up. We invited him to Larry's church and then
went on our way.

We stopped at a gas station and asked the young clerk
there if she went to church. She said she did and asked what
we were doing in town. We told her we were there to tell
people what Jesus has done for us. I invited her to come
to Larry's church and she asked us for a favor. She wanted
us to go see her dad since she didn't know if he was lost
or saved. She gave us the address and we headed over to

his house. When we arrived, we past hunting dogs laying in the yard and knocked on the door. The man that answered told us that his wife was a Baptist minister and that when he goes to church, it's usually with her. We thanked him for his time and got back in our car. I turned to Ken and said that this didn't make sense to me; that couldn't have been the young girl's Dad. We drove back to the main street and stopped at the first house we saw. When we knocked, a boy answered the door followed by his 35 to 40 year old mother. We invited her to Larry's church and suddenly she started crying uncontrollably. I said, "I hope I didn't say anything to hurt you." She told us that she had just gotten out of jail and while in there, she had befriended a Christian woman who made her promise to go to church. The poor woman was dumbfounded and didn't know what to think. She had made this promise two days ago and now I showed up. I told her, "That's the way God works." When Sunday came, Larry asked me if we knew the people on the back row. I turned and there was the woman who had just gotten out of jail with her two children. Her boyfriend was there, too; he was the man from City Hall. And next to him was his daughter. There are no accidents with God.

*On Oct. 31, 2002, I was in the hospital. I was very sick and wasn't getting any better or any answers. I tried to call my doctor from the hospital room, and thank God, the line was busy. I slammed the phone down so hard it should have broken the phone or the table it was sitting on. I then screamed at God as loud as I could. "If you want me take me, if you want me out of here, fine. I will do whatever you want me to do." That was seven years to the day that my brother almost died in a hospital. That was when I truly surrendered to the Lord Jesus Christ.

*I was baptized a second time in the spring of 2003. I was ordained a deacon in June of 2003. I was working at the cabin gathering wood for the winter in the fall of 2005.

As I was putting wood under the porch, I was bent over and God called me to preach. I laid the wood down and I called Vickie and told her. I told her I thought maybe God wanted me to preach. I could drive Pastor Leroy and help out at other churches if he couldn't make it by himself.

*On one of our trips by freighter, we stopped in Hong Kong Harbor and were told of a street market that was open at night. We got directions from a crewmember who told us what bus that we needed to get on to find the correct street. While on the bus, there was a commotion at the back of the bus and we tried to find out why the people seemed to be very angry. We tried to find someone who spoke English to tell us what the problem was. A young girl told us that someone had stolen her identity. At that time, many boat people were coming into the country and needed identity cards. We asked her where we were going and she said to the police station. When we got there and they opened the door of the bus, we just walked off. They were not interested in us because we had no reason to steal an identity from anyone. As we left the bus, we asked a policeman where the street was that we were looking for and he said we were only 2 blocks from there.

HATE

"But I say unto you, Love your enemies, bless them that curse you, do good to them that hate you, and pray for them which despitefully use you, and persecute you." Matthew 5:44

✱I went to the Baptist church up the road from my river cabin on a Wednesday night. About eight other people had come for the service. I took a seat and the preacher said, "Tonight we are going to be talking about hate." I knew that God had brought me to that church. This was around the time I was speaking in many churches about how I got rid of the hate that possessed me for seven years.

*The day came for Pastor Leroy to be moved out of ICU. I told Alice, the cleaning lady we had befriended, that we wouldn't be coming back. I asked her if she wanted to hear my testimony and she said yes. I shared my story with her and ended with the fact that with the love of Jesus Christ, I was set free from all hate. Alice then shared with me about a woman she worked with at the hospital who was not very pleasant. As time went by, she and the other woman, who never really got along, started avoiding each other. One day, Alice said something came over her and she walked straight up to the other woman, said, "I'm sorry," and gave her a hug. Alice knew that she had been set free and now the two of them get along fine. Alice offered me a hug and a thank you as we left.

*In the fall in Missouri, I take my cab-over camper and head out of town to deer hunt. While out of town, I try and find a new church to attend on Wednesday nights. One such trip took me to a small community church that was having a revival with an out of town evangelist. The church was full, but I find the seats up front are usually empty, so I headed straight there. When the preacher started, he asked how many born again Christians were there. I knew I liked this guy because he was finding out what's important. About 80 % had their hands up. He then asked how many of the Christians had been responsible for bringing one or two people to Christ. I looked around and saw several hands go up. He then asked how many of us brought five people to Christ. Not many hands were still up. Then he asked how many of us had brought ten people to Christ. Only two hands were visible. When asked if we brought fifteen people to Christ, no hands went up. Something inside me snapped and I jumped up and pulled my business card out that reads, "God Spoke To Me, Willing To Share My Testimony, Anytime, Any Place." I took the card and went to the pulpit and slapped it down and said, "I don't know how many people I have brought to Christ because I'm just a seed sower!" When I turned around, about 150 eyes were on me. I started my testimony about how God called my name and how Jesus pulled me out of the pit of Hell and I saw the light of Heaven. I turned back to the preacher and apologized for taking over his service. He was grinning ear-to-ear and said, "Don't ever apologize when the Holy Sprit comes on you." At that, I went back and sat down. The preacher said he wanted everyone to know that he had never seen me before and that this was no act and he went on to preach a very strong sermon. When I moved to the door to leave, two ladies came up and said that they thought God brought me to their church and was glad I came.

VICKIE'S VIEW

I don't know how many other women have been married over 50 years to a man who was changed so completely by a vision. He (Ken) has always been intensely focused on whatever he was doing. That part of him has not changed. We have probably constructed over 300 homes in our career days. We worked hard, then, took time off, traveling on freighters and driving around Australia and New Zealand several times. We have had many adventures as we traveled around the world seeing the wonders of nature first hand. Although Ken strayed into the worldly arena, I tried to be faithful to Jesus Christ in church attendance, Sunday school teaching, Bible reading and prayer. Ken is now a man who not only talks the talk of Jesus and His saving power, but he walks the walk as best as he can. He visits the sick and widows and travels anywhere he is invited to share the gospel and to lift people up by his testimony of God's love and grace to all.

AFTER THOUGHTS

A s I look back, I can see that God had His loving hand on my entire life. I was born in a house just four blocks from the church I attend now. Growing up, I never heard about God unless I said something about Him that was wrong and then Mom and Dad would come down hard on me. Dad would occasionally talk about church. As I think back now, I wonder if they were mad at God for taking my brother when he was a baby.

My grandma took me to the Assembly of God Church when I was about five years old. Sixty years later, I spoke in that very same church after God called my name. My mother sent my brothers and me to Sunday school one time at the First Baptist Church. I remember they gave me a picture of Jesus with sheep standing around Him. I spoke at that church sixty years later as well.

The little grocery store that was at 902 Arkansas, near my childhood home, became the Second Baptist Church of Rolla, Missouri. Everett Hunt lived right across the street from the store when it closed down. I believe he might have had a hand in making the building into a church. In the 50's, my mom and dad started attending. I was baptized in that church and when I was first saved, it was Everett who walked up to me and said, "I have prayed for you for years."

I spoke in a church the other night about Satan tempting Jesus in Matthew 4:8, 9. Satan took Jesus up on a high mountain and showed Him all the beauty of the world. He told Jesus He could have it all if He would bow down to Satan and worship Him. That shows how stupid Satan is. Jesus created and owned it all anyway. My point is this: when I left the church and went around seeing the world, I had worldly problems. I started getting sick and I got a rash that wouldn't go away. I broke ribs, my leg, and a bone in my back and my hand several times. When I got back into the church, my troubles disappeared for the most part. When I was in my 40's, I told Vickie that I wanted to travel now and work later. Little did I know that my work wouldn't be building houses. It would be getting out spreading the Word of God, going door-to-door, house-to-house, and hospital-to-hospital. I use my travels now to talk with people from other states and countries about Jesus Christ.

I knew one man that said to me that his son never calls or talks to him. He feels that his son doesn't care about him. That's what God thinks if we never go to Him in prayer. It says in Revelations 3:20, "Behold I stand at the door and knock. If any man hears my voice and opens the door, I will come in to him and will sup with him and he with me."

FINAL THOUGHTS

As I finish this book, I realize that it's not because of *my* strength that it was written. The strength is from God. The book was written for one reason only: for the lost to be brought to Jesus Christ. The first thing you have to know is Romans 3:23, "For all have sinned and come short of the glory of God." The next thing is to repent, to turn around from your sin and go the other way. Then you must know Romans 6:23, "For the wages of sin is death, but the gift of God is eternal life through Jesus Christ our Lord." The Bible says in Ephesians 2:8, 9, "For by grace you are saved through faith, and that not of yourself, it is the gift of God. Not of works, lest any man should boast."

These are the things that will keep you out of Hell. A lot of people believe that just because they are good and do good things, that God won't let them go to Hell. This is true to a certain point. God does not send anyone to Hell. It is a choice for man to make, either Heaven or Hell.

That's what this book is all about. Love God with all your heart, mind and soul. Love your neighbor as yourself. These are the most important commands. I had a true turning point in my life and I now know what a true Christian should be. I try to always treat people with kindness and compas-

sion. I try to be available for people in their time of need.
Just like Jesus has always been for me.

I have been born again! Praise God.

CPSIA information can be obtained at www.ICGtesting.com
Printed in the USA
BVOW082352250712

296089BV00001B/5/P